Helping Public Schools
Bridging the Gap

(Bonus)
Ideas on Parental Involvement
& Community Outreach

"Armadillo Jim" Schmidt

HELPING PUBLIC SCHOOLS
© 2006 by Jim Schmidt

Published by Golden Faith Books
Tulsa, Oklahoma

ISBN 10: 0-9716689-3-0
ISBN 13: 978-0-9716689-3-5

Cover
Mach Rock Productions
Blake Markham

Editing
SRS Graphics
Sheila Schmidt

Typesetting
Charlene Panak

Printed in the United States of America

For information:
jim@armadillojim.com
www.helpingpublicschools.com

Dedication

To my darling wife Sheila, my family and all the teachers, educators, counselors, fair managers, ministers, business leaders, friends, donors and anyone who helped me see over three million children with my pet armadillos, I dedicate this book to you. You get the credit for helping us reach more children now. We also want to give a special thank you to Charlene Panak who volunteered countless hours in typesetting this book. You made us look good.

To my luggage looking pets, thanks for sharing your armor!

To God, for giving me His full armor.

If an armadillo can get into over 1000 schools, you can too!

Contents

From the Author

More than 25 years ago, my pet armadillos and I started visiting schools. In my first assembly, presented in an elementary school, I talked about dinosaurs, biology and wildlife, just about any subject I thought related to armadillos. Although at that time way back in 1980, I was very comfortable with adult audiences, being a relatively new public speaker, I was a bit nervous among these school children because they were not my peers. Most were young, between 6 to 11 years old. Yet, when I presented my pet armadillos to those students in that first school, I became excited. These children were focused and so very interested in what I had to say. They were inquisitive and mesmerized in seeing a live armadillo. Many students had never seen or much less touched an armadillo. The questions these children asked were thoughtful and curious. I'll never forget that day at St. Peter and Paul Catholic School in New Braunfels, Texas.

Now, more than 1000 schools later, that little presentation with an armadillo has grown into a non-profit foundation called, *Put On Your Armor*™. My pet armadillos and I, along with many volunteers and docents have seen over three million children, "armoring" them with love against drugs, crime and violence. I'm sure glad I chose an animal that looked like luggage because we have traveled millions of miles.

Today, we are seeing a new kind of student in this current school generation. These children are still asking good questions, however they are severely distracted in their quest for knowledge.

Students now are much more challenged by problems in schools like drugs, bullying and inadequate nutrition. Other education barriers include social ills, funding cuts, teacher shortages, dangerous and disruptive home lives and immoral and misleading messages from television, society and the internet. Today, parental breakups, transient lifestyles and the severe mental and emotional casualties of disasters, trauma and displacement shatter many children's hopes and dreams.

Helping Public Schools is a way to keep children on the road to better education and in the path God created for each special child.

There is no one perfect solution in *Helping Public Schools* but when you take action, you'll find the rewards will benefit you, your community, organization and most importantly the generation to follow.

America's public schools currently enroll more than 45,000,000 students in grades Kindergarten through 12th. More than 100,000 campuses and schools offer facilities like gyms, stadiums, classrooms, cafeterias and other space where you will form relationships and present programs that will make a difference in the lives of our greatest resource, children. These programs will also impact your life and that of the members in your organization.

In this book you will glean over 25 years of experience and ideas on how to effectively reach the harvest fields and human resources found in America's public schools.

Like you, I just wanted to make a difference in the lives of young people. Frankly, I just love children. Today, I am asking you to join other Americans in rolling up your sleeves and taking an active role in bringing hope and healing to our children.

Please, for the sake of children, become a believer in what you can do in *Helping Public Schools*. All it takes is action. You will increase your influence and significance when you take action. Just dive in because there is a school of 45,000,000 fish waiting to be caught!

Before you get started, I'd like to share one funny story about what happened in a public school recently. While interviewing a student at the front of the audience during a drug prevention assembly I was conducting, I looked down to see that the ten-year-old had his left shoe on his right foot and his right shoe on his left foot. I looked at the shoes and then looked back up to him . . . then back to the shoes, then  to the audience then back up to his eyes. I did this several times until I finally asked: *"Do you have your shoes on the right feet?"* He looked down and without missing a beat he answered; "Yes sir, these are my feet"!

In *Helping Public Schools* you'll enable thousands of students to get started on the right foot. As it is written, "How beautiful are the feet of those who bring good news!" Romans 10:15.

Introduction

The purpose of this book is to bridge the gap to public schools and to call you to action. Hopefully, it will motivate you, your church, business, civic club and family from just talking about problems in public schools to taking an active role in making a positive difference. Thereby, you will increase your influence and significance.

This book is a great reference guide or equipment manual for any pastor, ceo, business owner, community relations executive, civic leader, ordinary citizen or interested parent who wants to make a difference in the lives of children in public schools and your community.

Helping Public Schools is a tool and manual for anyone interested in today's children and the American education system. This book offers helpful ways, projects and ideas for you to get involved and call others to action.

Before you endeavor any of the 101 action steps, first do what is most important, which is, develop a relationship with a teacher, principal, bus driver, custodian, coach or someone at the public school nearest your work or home. If you are a parent with children in school, get involved and then double your efforts by recruiting others to help you make a difference in your children's school.

> *"Change a child's environment and you'll change that child's mind!"*

Why is Helping Public Schools Your Responsibility?

The most famous and most read book says: *"Train up a child in the way he (she) should go and when he is old he will not depart from it"* (Proverbs 22:6).

Training and helping children is everyone's responsibility. It is your responsibility. The next time you get change from a young clerk at a grocery store or the next time a young mechanic works on the jet engine of the plane you are flying, or the youthful policeman answers your distress call, remember that you may have had a hand in raising that person. Your associates in the workplace and members of your church all went to school. Your friends and most of your children's and grandchildren's friends and future mates are products of public schools.

> *"A man of words and not of deeds is like a garden full of weeds."*
> *Shirley Kelly*

Everyone is responsible for raising children. Responsibility begins at birth with parents and moves to other family members and then to the community. Today's churches and businesses must take the lead in helping public schools stimulate the valuable resources, creativity and assets offered by our most energetic citizens, children. In *Helping Public Schools* you will find enrichment, innovative community and parental involvement and a potential for creating a country full of newly trained leaders, parents, workers and educators.

Unless everyone does their part, our next generation will fall short of today's generation in terms of wages, education, social skills and productivity.

Helping Public Schools is the answer to America's greatest test. What grade will you make and what will you tell your grandchildren when they ask, "What did you do to help public schools?" The very least we can give our children and grandchildren is hope. Your help will give children that hope! So, are you helping public schools yet?

"A man of words and not of deeds is like a garden full of weeds." Shirley Kelley, a sweet little lady from Cameron, Texas said this while raising five children. Shirley served on school boards, was president of her church *Women's United* and served on the *Cameron City Council.*

Author's Note: Many times church pastors or club presidents call to invite me to visit their city and visit schools on their behalf. I always tell them that I will be honored to come to their city provided they can pass my three question test.

1. What is the name of the school nearest your church or club?
2. What is the principal's name nearest your church or club?
3. What is more important, building relationships or getting your name in front of the public?

As You Get Started

It would be helpful to know about the *Equal Access Act*, which addresses religion or faith in schools. Keep in mind however, that most of the programs and ideas found in this book have nothing to do with Equal Access because they are not part of any curriculum or official school activity or do not involve direct participation from students. The ideas in this book increase your influence and significance, thus giving you increased access to students, teachers and their families. Still, you would be wise to know your rights and especially the rights of students. Information on the *Equal Access Act* can be found at the back of the book on page 87.

Helping Public Schools

101 Ways to Bridge the Gap.

−1−
Pray for your community, students, administrators and teachers daily

Prayer was never removed from public schools. In the U.S. Supreme court cases cited in 1962 and 1963 it is clear that the rulings only prohibit forced or teacher initiated prayer. Any student or teachers may pray silently or audibly, just as one would have a conversation and provided it is not disruptive to any class activity. **Students are "legally" allowed to pray in America's public schools.** Throughout history, prayer was a daily part of public school activity. For more information about students' religious rights in schools visit Jay Sekulow's *American Center for Law and Justice* at www.aclj.org or Brad Dacus at www.pacificjustice.org.

For educators another good resource is the *Christian Educators Association International* whose web address is www.ceai.org.

Each year the United States commemorates Religious Freedom Day. The President declares January 16th to be Religious Freedom Day and calls upon Americans to "observe this day through appropriate events and activities in homes, schools and places of worship." The day is the anniversary of the passage, in 1786, of the Virginia Statute of Religious Freedom. The goal of Religious Freedom Day is to promote and protect students' religious expression rights by informing educators, parents and students about these liberties.

You can order merchandise promoting this event and give some of these items as gifts to educators. Ask the librarian and principal to post the presidential proclamation in the library or classroom. Visit the Religious Freedom Day website at: www.religiousfreedomday.com.

Additionally, the first Thursday of May is National Day of Prayer. This day has been set aside and authorized by an act of our United States Congress. Why not ask your members to gather at a public school on the First Thursday of May. Visit the National Day of Prayer website. Donate and post National Day of Prayer posters in the schools and deliver one to each school board member. Visit www.ndptf.org. Speakers are also available.

Also, remember to gather on the special Wednesday in September when students unite in front of their school's flag pole during the annual prayer event called See You At the Pole. A follow-up program in your community called See You At the Party is also recommended. Please visit their website at www.syatp.com.

Also available is the paperback resource and wonderful prayer guide from Harrison House Publishing titled; *Praying for Our Nation.* Visit their website at www.harrisonhouse.com.

You can also enroll in the national prayer movement, *Raise Your Hand,* for educators and schools sponsored and endorsed by the *Christian Educators Association International.*

Also contact another prayer network called *Schoolife*. Contact information for both can be found at www.schoolife.org or www.raiseyourhand.us.

Below are two suggested prayers to use each day or week. Forward these prayers to your friends or prayer team. Form a school prayer team.

Dear God,

Thank you for our local schools. Thank you for our teachers, principals, superintendents, volunteers, bus drivers, custodians, parents, coaches, staff, parents and most importantly the students. We ask for your wisdom in directing all of these and especially the students in the way they should go. We pray for safety and an environment rich in knowledge and understanding and openness to God's truth found in His word. Help all who are searching for you find you today, especially those in public schools in Jesus' name, Amen.

Dear God,

I plead the blood of Jesus over my sins and the sins of this nation. Lord, send revival and end abortion in Jesus Name, Amen.

Author's Note: As a direct result of Roe vs. Wade and abortion, over 45 million students have been erased from public schools. That is equal to all students in America's public schools this year. Imagine empty schools in America! Contact *Bound-4-Life;* http://bound4life.com or the *National Right to Life;* www.nrlc.org about their campaigns to end abortion in America.

—2—
Donate Bibles to public school students

Many students in our public schools today do not own a Bible. *The Gideon's* are a good resource in obtaining Bibles or partnering in this outreach. They will help you by putting you in touch with a local chapter to help you get this done. Contact *The Gideon's* at www.gideons.org.

—3—
Start a *Kids for Christ* Bible Club www.kfcusa.org (918) 902-2442 (Tulsa, Oklahoma)

Kids for Christ USA, www.kfcusa.org a non-profit 501-c-3 will assist any school, business or church in any community in any city in America in establishing Bible clubs and/or Bible lessons in public schools. These clubs generally meet "before or after the bell". Students and their parents initiate these volunteer-led Bible clubs. *Kids for Christ* will help train and advise local *KFC* clubs. *KFC* club tee shirts, games, sermons and lessons/curriculum are available. Annual training seminars are held in Tulsa, Oklahoma. The values learned in these programs affect students learning ability, attitude, stress level and relationships. In a recent survey conducted by *KFC* a majority of the students replied that *KFC* helped improve their school day, find a friend and that their overall grades were better. Many *KFC* clubs have become ministries within the schools. One club sponsored the headstone of a student whose parents couldn't afford one following their child's death. Another club made a turkey dinner and other meals for another family in time of grief. Another *KFC* club collected back to school backpacks as a Hurricane Katrina relief effort. What other program enriches the learning environment like *Kids for Christ*? Visit www.kfcusa.org.

Author's Note: I lead one of the local *Kids for Christ* clubs each week. This is one of the most rewarding volunteer efforts of my life in public schools. The children are so hungry for God's word. Over 50 percent of the students who attend my club which meets before the Wednesday morning bell, say that this is their only form of church.

Jenks Journal
A Community Publishers, Inc. newspaper

Back to school with the Bible
By Don Diehl
Journal Editor

So you've heard about the Bible being banned from public schools, right?

"Not true," says area resident Bob Heath who heads up a national organization called *Kids for Christ USA.*

"As students start back to class in area schools this month, Heath is ready to help parents and students organize Bible clubs in their schools in the Tulsa-Jenks-Broken Arrow, OK area.

Heath helped start nearly three dozen such clubs in Oklahoma in 2001, and the model is now being used from New York to California.
This year he will assist other parent-student groups in Jenks as well as help students launch new

clubs where the Bible is studied and its principles practiced.

Kids for Christ USA has seen thousands of children not only come to know Jesus, but have learned during the weekly meetings how to share their faith and Christian lifestyle with friends and family members.

But Heath also is on another mission to rid the myth that the Christian faith must stop at the schoolhouse door.

If that was true, Heath says, then not only has the Bible been banned but constitutional rights as well.

"We hear a lot about how the government Bible, prayer and witnessing has been removed from the public schools, but its a lie," he said. "

The year I was born: 1963, was the year that one of the greatest media spins in history began," he said. "The belief that the Bible and prayer were removed from the schools."

Heath says that people are not clear on the difference of two words mandatory and voluntary. He said that the 1963 ruling deals with government mandating school prayer, but even though there may be objections, voluntary prayer, carrying and studying the Bible and other expressions of faith aren't only to be allowed, they are protected.

In 1963, Heath said he has learned, Madeline Murray-O'Hare won the right for her son and others to opt out of mandatory Bible reading and prayer.

"That is a far cry from the media spin and intimidation we have bought for 43 years," he said.

"It is time we in the church begin to publicize the truth and stop propagating this lie.

Heath said the result of the "spin" has been catastrophic because the Bible and prayer is removed from the lives of many of America's children.

"I remember vividly feeling like I would be suspended if I even admitted being a Christian, let alone shared my faith with a friend," Heath said.

According to the *Family Research Council*, the 1984 *Equal Access Act* (EAA) requires schools to grant religious student groups the same rights and privileges as non-religious student groups. Though some Christian organizations have been challenged for hosting Bible clubs in public schools, Heath said he hasn't received any significant opposition. He said he spoke with a representative of the *American Center for Law and Justice* in the developmental stages of *KFC* to make sure he was on solid legal ground.

If you'd like to get involved with KFCUSA, contact Heath at (918)902-2442 or at bobheath@fcusa.org.

Printed by permission Jenks Journal

Author's Note: Though the thief tried to steal God's word from our public schools through Madalyn Murray O'Hair , her son, William J. Murray is now helping restore Religious Freedom in America. For booking and other information visit the Religious Freedom Coalition at www.rfcnet.org

Another organization which is bringing the Bible back to schools as curriculum and which is predominantly in secondary schools is The *National Council on Bible Curriculum in Public Schools* or NCBCPS headed by President and Founder, Elizabeth Ridenour and endorsed by Mr. and Mrs. Chuck Norris. Learn all you can about NCBCPS at their web site: www.bibleinschools.net.

A third and most effective Bible outreach in secondary public schools is the *Bible Literacy Project*. Visit www.bibleliteracy.org.

Using an innovative textbook titled, *The Bible and Its Influence*, the *Bible Literacy Project* is a *First Amendment Safe* curriculum covering Genesis to Revelation. The goal of the program is to bring an academic study of the Bible to public high schools as an English or social studies elective. Endorsed by scholars and theologians everywhere, this program is the answer to student's rights and their desire to study the Bible as an elective during a school day. Order the textbook and obtain more information at: www.bibleliteracy.org.

Child Evangelism Fellowship offers after school Bible clubs called the *Good News Club*. Contact them at www.cefonline.com.

—4—
Drive a school bus

Millions of students ride the school bus to and from school each day. The average ride is 20-30 minutes depending on the geographic area. Greeting a student in a positive and godly way can make all the difference to a child. One church in Oklahoma City attributed its growth to the fact that their senior pastor drove a school bus. When interviewed, one church member said that his family chose the church because their middle school daughter kept saying, "Today Pastor said this, or today Pastor said that". Finally, the dad asked his daughter, "Where do you keep hearing this Pastor?" "Oh, he is my bus driver," she said.

Encourage your fellow workers, members and associates to get certified, CDL driver training so they too can drive a bus and subsequently touch more lives.

Author's Note: It is better to have an audience twice a day on a mobile church (bus) than to hope and pray for one for Sunday morning. Fish where the fish are!

—5—

Adopt-a-School

Many churches and organizations today are partners with their local public schools through a program called, *Adopt-a-School*. Contrary to popular belief, these partnerships are not limited to businesses and civic clubs. Schools desperately need help with supplies, mentoring programs, staffing, funding and other resources.

Dr. Tony Evans of Dallas, Texas and founder of *The Urban Alternative* has developed a comprehensive faith-based strategy, *National Church Adopt-A-School Initiative, (NCAASI)*, to address the spiritual and social needs of urban youth and families through a church and public school partnership based on the Dallas, Texas *Project Turn •Around* (PTA) model.

The *National Church Adopt-A-School Initiative,* or *NCAASI* strategy, along with several other outreach strategies, has been packaged into a 500-page hand-out. *Project Turn•Around* Implementation Toolkit for replication in your church and community.

Dr. Evans' website: www.TonyEvans.org states the following: "*Project Turn•Around* is a social outreach with the mission to rebuild communities from the inside out with a comprehensive faith-based program designed to improve and enrich the lives of urban youth and families. It is our conviction that true change must come from the inside out. Therefore, in order to impact lives, we must address the moral and spiritual foundations upon which those lives are built, while simultaneously meeting felt needs.

It is our conviction that the church, not the government, is the best social delivery system since it is closer to the needs of people, offers the largest potential volunteer force, already has facilities for impact programs and offers a moral and spiritual frame of reference for making right choices.

When churches develop a Kingdom perspective, they cease being ingrown and then are free to mobilize volunteers to meet the crying needs of urban young people while strengthening their family structure in a context of compassion, moral training and spiritual accountability. *Project Turn•Around* provides a hand-up, not a hand-out. *Project Turn•Around* provides holistic long-term, not short-term solutions, by meeting needs in a way that changes how people think, which ultimately determines how they live."

Contact Dr. Tony Evans and the *National Church Adopt-A-School Initiative*, (NCAASI) through their website: www.tonyevans.org or call (800) 800-3222.

Many churches have joined other adopt a school partnerships promoted within their own school districts. Contact your local superintendent or school principal to ask how to join the *Adopt-a-School* partnership.

—6—
Adopt a Teacher/Educator/Principal of the Year

Most communities or school districts have an adopt-a-school or adopt-a-teacher program in which your organization can become an active participant or local sponsor. By becoming a partner to a school in your community, you will provide valuable resources to students and teachers. Most schools participate in the *National Teacher of the Year* program beginning at the local level.

Usually, the *Teacher of the Year* program in your state already works with many regional and state sponsors. Find out who these sponsors are and partner with them and other businesses to localize prizes for schools/teachers nearest your church or business. Organize a group of businesses, churches or clubs under one umbrella sponsorship, always remembering that there is strength in numbers and a great blessing in unity. Retailers, restaurants and other independent businesses are always willing to partner in programs like the *Teacher of the Year*. A local restaurant in Tulsa, Oklahoma offers a Teachers Appreciation Certificate for Teacher Appreciation Week. There are many ways to enhance this program which may include contacting a local car dealership to partner with them to give away a car (or use of) each year.

Remember to invite your local and state *Teacher of the Year* winners to address your congregation or company so you can honor them after the award winners are announced and while they are on tour promoting the campaign. Former *State Teachers of the Year* are available to advise you too. Contact your school district for specific local contact information and calendar of events. Visit their website at www.ccsso.org/projects/national_teacher_of_the_year (spaces have underscore).

Christian Educators Association International also hosts an *Educator / Teacher of the Year* program recognizing and equipping both public and private school teachers. Visit this excellent program at: www.ceai.org.

Principals are recognized annually by the *National Association of Secondary School Principals*. Visit the *National Principal of the Year* website at: www.principals.org.

Always remember to promote this sponsorship and any other event or annual activity you sponsor by adding the information to your organization's and facility's signage or commercial vehicles i.e.: *XYZ Proud Sponsor of the State Teacher of the Year*.

−7−

Sponsor special appreciation gifts and/or banquets:

There are dozens of occasions where your organization can greatly influence a school or be a significant participant of a school event or special occasion. The following list suggests many tried and affective programs.

- Teacher appreciation gifts or banquet

Sponsoring teacher gift baskets and/or flowers or a banquet are some of the most effective ways to build relationships and affect change in the school. Teachers can use many helpful items like book bags made of canvas, day timers and necessities like Kleenex®, paper towels and other classroom accessories. You can place your logo or scripture verse on the bags or other items you donate. As a suggestion, poinsettias make lovely Christmas gifts. Some retailers sell these for only $2.00 and offer a space on the wrapper to place your name. There are dozens of ideas for special occasions. Don't forget the obvious gifts like lotions, cleansing liquids, candles and potpourri. One church encourages its members to adopt a teacher and supplement his/her income, or pay for continuing education and supplies. As an added show of appreciation, show up to school early one morning a week, (being very consistent) with fresh fruit and/or flowers. While you are washing and cutting the fruit or preparing the flower arrangement in the teacher's lounge, you will meet teachers and share some one-on-one time. Leave a calling card: *Compliments of XYZ.* This technique is very effective for salesmen so it will certainly work for you at any school. More ideas and info can be found by visiting www.nea.org/teacherday.

- Bus driver appreciation gifts or banquet

School bus drivers, over 400,000 nationally, are the most underpaid and most responsible of all public school staff. Drivers transport America's most valuable assets and cargo, children, into some of the most dangerous conditions and locations in America, yet have not been recognized as heroes in most communities. One bus driver in north Florida once said, "*If someone ever bought me a dinner for driving their kids to school every day, it would be a first. We never get recognition and yet sometimes we are the first ones to know if they have a problem*". Bus drivers are the first line of defense for children. In many school districts, the bus driver is the first and last school representative a student sees each day. Bus drivers sometimes serve as counselors, disciplinarians and mediators. Many drivers are the eyes and ears or "watchdogs" of a child's home and their neighborhood. Bus drivers are the first to know if a child's front door has been kicked in, their cat got run over, the electricity has been turned off or if mama got a new car. Bus drivers have special needs like the all-important cell phone, sunglasses, gas cardholders, alarm clocks, lunch boxes, whistles, key chains, flashlights, air gauges, walkie-talkies, bullhorns and special apparel like rain gear, gloves, caps and coats.

Sometimes just an appreciation note goes a long way. Learn as much as you can about this industry, partnership ideas, sponsorship and drivers at www.schoolbusfleet.com.

> **Author's Note:** Obtain a certified drivers license, (CDL) and encourage your associates to do the same. Become a bus driver in your community. Meet at the bus barn to drive your mobile church. "Better to reach an audience two times a day than hope for one on Sunday!"

- Custodian or maintenance staff appreciation gifts or banquet

Custodian appreciation gifts or banquets are another great way to reach into your schools. Custodians have such important jobs. Custodians hold the keys to the school. Custodians or as some still call, janitors, are often the first on the scene/job following a tragedy, riot, or student incident like vomit on the floor, a spill or breakage or even a fight. Remember that custodians are entrusted with the keys to the school. Custodians generally have more direct contact with students than a principal or teacher does. Custodians have special needs like shoes, tools, key holders, equipment, toolboxes, mop buckets and more. Contact a local or national janitorial supply distributor to purchase professional custodian-type items. Also, organize annual, quarterly or monthly Custodian or Janitor Appreciation and Helper Days when you can assemble members of your organization (like a division of your company or men's club at your church) at the school to clean, organize and repair property. You can also extend this to the grounds crew to help in cleanup, garbage pickup and landscaping or lawn service. Perhaps one day you will have these key people in organizations like *Custodians for Christ* or *Janitors for Jesus*. A thank you note, a complimentary dinner and a pat on the back will have major influence.

- Coaches appreciation gifts or banquet

One of the most influential leaders in the school is the coach or physical education instructor. These role models' and leaders' time are often stretched with other teaching responsibilities. Helping with booster clubs, equipment acquisition and other sports related duties are helpful. Provide coaches with their own personal training duffel bags complete with special items like razors, cologne, socks and a grooming kit. Place your logo on some of the items and include a card letting them know you are cheering for them. Remember to add a small pocket Bible! Treat these coaches or staff to a meal or special banquet, or weekend retreat exclusively tailored for their taste and lifestyles. Once in a while just send them a gift certificate to their favorite restaurant.

Author's Note: *Crossings Church* of Oklahoma City hosts an annual day called *Bridging the Gap*. This year, during the week prior to back to school, over 400 church members visited seven public school campuses in this most recent one-day event. In addition to cleanup, painting and repair projects, the church youth group painted the state seal on the concrete of one school's entrance. The media covered the event where many school administrators were also on hand to say "thank you" to church members! For more detailed information contact *Crossings Community Church* at www.crossingsokc.org/ministries/missions/bridge.html.

- Police / Security Officers appreciation gifts or banquet

  These men and women deserve a 'thank you' They will really appreciate any recognition and gifts. Host a banquet for the security officers, *DARE* officers and neighborhood patrol officers. Present appreciation notes from students, certificates, memorable photos and other gifts. An additional appreciation letter to their chief goes a long way.

- Counselors appreciation gifts or banquet

  A counselor has great impact on students anytime but especially during a time of need. Creating good relationships with counselors will help them help your child and other students. Visit *Focus on the Family,* www.family.org for more help and resources for counselors. Also visit the *American Association of Christian Counselors* at www.aacc.net or the *National Christian Counselors Association* at: www.ncca.org.

  Your state educational system also has organizations exclusively reaching school counselors. Visit your state education website for more contact information.

- Principals appreciation gifts or banquet

  Principals are the authority figures and the leaders students see when there is a problem. Whether in disciplining, correcting or helping, the principal will be better equipped to go the extra-mile for your child and others students when you have taken the time to establish a relationship and good will. Take a principal to lunch. Visit the www.principals.org website for other sponsorship opportunities.

- Cooks/chefs appreciation gesture

Purchase personally monogrammed aprons, mittens, hot pads, towels and other items. Add a scripture or other positive message (i.e.: *"Man can not live by bread alone"*). Encourage members of your organization to create and sew aprons. Collect and publish recipes from the cooks at your local school and highlight these winning recipes in an annual award ceremony, television or news feature. Everybody likes to eat and talk about food. What about a special chili supper event, a progressive dinner to each school, or another theme event? Why not consider sponsoring your school's cook to an all expense paid trip to a culinary school for a week? Or, sponsor a *Top Chef* to visit your city for a special night recognizing your school cooks. Contact the *National Association of Restaurant Owners* at www.restaurant.org or such companies like *Campbell's* makers of *Pace®* picante and *Campbell's Soup®* for more ideas and ways to promote your school's cooks and chefs. You can learn more on their website at www.cooksinschools.org.

Remember to order "take out" for the school once a year, thus giving the cooks a paid day off! Contact the local *Chic-Fil-A®* or your other local restaurants to help in this project.

- School crossing guard appreciation gifts or banquet/party. This event will be geared to the age appropriateness of the crossing volunteers. You may want to select a local pizza parlor or water park for the event for younger guards.

- School secretary's appreciation gifts and luncheons. These important staff members are considered the key to the door for most organizations. When you win favor with the school secretary, your efforts will be greatly enhanced. Try finding out the secretary's birthday or employment anniversary to mark these special occasions.

- *PTA*, volunteer coordinator and volunteers appreciation gifts or luncheons

- Superintendent's appreciation gifts or banquet.

- School board members appreciation gifts or banquet

- School nurse appreciation gifts or banquet

- Cheerleader, drum major, team captains, drill/flag team leaders , student council officers, class leaders, *ROTC* commanders, *FFA* and *4-H* and all other club leaders appreciation gifts and lunches.

- Sponsor student council and class officers appreciation gifts or leadership luncheon. You can learn more about this organization and how to maximize your influence by visiting the *National Association of Student Councils* website at: www.nasc.us.

Also, consider providing leadership tools featuring your logo and insignia such as: John Maxwell's or Myles Munroe's leadership books. Another great book is *Leadership and Self Deception*, a BK-published book. Other suggested gifts include John Mason's books such as his popular, *An Enemy Called Average*. Bob Harrison's books on increase or

Nasir Siddiki's books on wisdom are terrific resources for any students (see resource section for contact information).

Host a special leadership lunch with the mayor and civic leaders, state representatives and congressmen. Your student leaders will be greatly affected by the influence of your local officials and various gifts and educational resources. Invite some of the above authors to speak at the leadership luncheon or conference.

– 7 –

Always remember to take care of the widows and orphans first in your local schools and community

You can contact the school principal or counselor to see how many widows and/or orphans are involved in the school. Then put together a special gift for them at a time of need or special anniversary. Showing you care can make all the difference. There are many projects you can do but one of the most important is being sure the widow's financial needs are met. You can help a broader group of widows or single moms with other events like hosting special clothes swaps or a sports equipment swap box or day at the school. Prepare special scholarship funds to help support fees and college tuition.

Remember to let the local high schools know that you are connected with *Crisis Pregnancy Centers* and are available to help in these unforeseen situations. Leave a hotline number at the school.

Author's Note: Look for my upcoming book: *Helping Single Moms; 101 Ways to Show Your True Religion.* See Number #45 for more information.

—8—
Find all resources available to reach your community and schools

When you touch the heart of people, you touch their lives. Most people don't care how much you know until they know how much you care. Three basic ways to reach people are through:

- Life events
- Ministry events
- Calendar events

An excellent resource for any such occasion is www.harvestresources.com. This site helps you find certificates, congratulatory letters, thank you notes and ideas on how to reach into the lives of ordinary people in your community and schools.

—9—
Join Partners in Education also known as Communities in Education

Many communities host this program which is often co-sponsored by the local Chamber of Commerce. One church recently sent its members to a local school one weekend to give the teacher's lounge an extreme makeover. When the teachers saw their new surroundings they were overjoyed. Can you imagine the positive attitude of the teachers and staff by something as simple as a newly decorated and remodeled lounge? This is definitely a project to promote on your commercial property like on your building or vehicles signage, on your website and through the media. Promote a partnership challenge or contest so other companies, suppliers, vendors and churches can get involved. For more ideas and information visit www.cisnet.org.

Author's Note: The Extreme Teachers Lounge Makeover is one of my favorite ideas!

—10—
Adopt the families and especially the children of deployed military personnel

Host a special military day in honor of these heroes. Invite local and regional representatives of the military to the school on behalf of your organization. The children need to hear and see the appreciation of the sacrifice they and their parent and/or relative is making for America. If the family does not own a large American flag, purchase one and present it as a gift on a special occasion, like a birthday or day of deployment or Veteran's Day.

—11—
Sponsor sports-related advertising space

Purchase space on a scoreboard, printed game mini-schedules, game programs and spaces on the fences, bleachers, infield, or concession stands. Have you thought of sponsoring the bleacher cushions? This will help your community and sports fans take a "load off". Include a prayer or appropriate sports invocation printed on the cushion. Remember to order your cushions in the school colors well before each season/sport.

−12−
Purchase ads in school bulletins, newsletters, annual photo journal, websites and school signs

Remember to also use your own sign on your property to help schools promote various campaigns and schedules. Remind drivers about paying attention to children at play in the summer or remind other passerby's of things like back to school registration dates, *PTA* meetings, sports schedules and school holidays. Be an added publicity arm for your local school, especially if you have signage near well traveled roads. Also, advertisement brings more money and helps the schools' events and campaigns.

−13−
Sponsor a clean up day on a public school campus

Pay special attention to the entrance, corridors and frontage roads. Consider painting the curbing, parking lot stripes and entryway. Maybe you can sponsor a work/carpentry/maintenance day on school campus coordinating this event with the school custodian and his staff. Repair necessary items and areas especially in the most used areas like the lunchrooms and restrooms or cleaning windows and other areas that don't get regular attention.

See # 6 Custodians Appreciation and visit the *Crossings Community Church* website to glean ideas from their annual *Bridging the Gap* school outreach at www.crossingsokc.org.

— 14 —
Host a back to school carnival on school property

Ask your members or associates to collect items like backpacks, paper, colors, scissors, glue, pens and pencils (see #21 section B for more ideas). Set up games and refreshments.

— 15 —
Host a halloween alternative on the school property or at your facility

Donate your used wardrobe/costumes of wholesome characters for halloween. Create a pumpkin patch at your facility or on the school property and give students an opportunity to enjoy a field trip there. Hide coupons or prizes inside or under the pumpkins like you would during an Easter egg hunt. Host a pumpkin-carving contest, donating pumpkins to the school and then awarding valuable prizes at the school.

— 16 —
Throw a party anytime for the school

Host special events during great American celebrations like National Ice Cream Day, National Watermelon Day, National Hot Dog Day, Hockey Season Opening, Surf's Up Day, Wheat Harvest and many others. Invite all students and their families to this special occasion at the school during the evening of the celebration day. Also, research the name of the school and host an annual event in honor of such. i.e.: Mark Twain Elementary School could have a riverboat theme, Ben Franklin Elementary could have a kite-flying theme,

George Washington Carver could give away free peanuts, Lincoln Middle School could host a hat contest or beard growing contest for dads. Remember to contact local businesses to help support these events and give away grand prizes sponsored by local and national companies.

—17—
Sponsor a speaker's bureau for parents and the community in the evenings at the public school

Be specific on relevant issues like:

- How to protect children on the internet
- How to start a neighborhood watch.
- How to prevent children from abduction
- How to guard children from predators
- How to choose the right sport/talent/lessons for your child
- Bereavement classes
- How to recognize addictions and your parental responsibility
- How to cope after divorce
- How to raise children as a single mom
- How to sell your home
- How to start a small business
- How to improve your marriage
- How to live debt-free
- How to prepare your tax forms
- English as a second language

—18—

Sponsor Veteran's Day and Patriotic programs in the school

Allow the veterans in your organization to spearhead this program. Donate flags to every student. Contact www.flags.com and the local VFW chapter, American Legion, Korean, Vietnam, Dessert Storm, or War in Iraq veteran's chapters, for their involvement. Veterans love to participate in flag raising ceremonies. Sponsor essay contests and award prizes for such. Many local businesses will donate prizes for this. Make sure to give supporters and partners adequate thanks and advertisement for their donations. Coordinate this with your local media and gain much exposure for the winners, veterans and your endeavor. Work with local Boy Scouts and Girl Scout leaders to cross promote various activities. See # 36 for more patriotic ideas.

Author's Note: I won the Voice of Democracy contest in high school. The *Daughters of the American Revolution* and great veterans groups can help you. Activities for *Boys State* and *Girls State*, the summer government interns program can be found at www.legion.org.

Remember to start or support a local girl scout or boy scout troop in the local school. Visit www.scouting.org or www.girlscouts.org.

—19—
Sponsor special Teacher Appreciation Week projects

Promote this special week by printing posters and displaying them at your church or business. Encourage members to donate to the project, make gifts or adopt a teacher for the week.

Teachers would love a free makeover session. Donate and sponsor professional hairstylists and makeover specialists. Conduct a drawing so teachers can win a massage and then send the massage therapist or trainer to the school for special sessions. You may also sponsor a drawing among all the local teachers where they will have a chance to win an all-expense paid trip to a resort spa. Contact resorts, airlines and travel agencies to get the best deal for such endeavor. These organizations may donate a trip or product in trade for advertising or publicity. There are many other things you can do including donating gift certificates, gift baskets and recognizing teachers through signage and advertising. Write a letter to a congressman or Governor asking for higher teacher pay and send a carbon copy to the teachers in your local schools on your letterhead of course.

Visit www.schoollife.org for more ideas on how to bless the teachers and educators in your public schools.

— 20 —

Donate backpacks, clothes, shoes, socks, gloves, coats and blankets to needy families and students

A church in Clovis, New Mexico hosts an annual back to school *Backpack & Coat Giveaway Day*. In this most recent event, parents lined up at the church as early as 6:00 a.m. to receive the items being distributed by the pastor and church volunteers. The press featured the event on the evening news.

— 21 —

Sponsor a drug/crime/violence-prevention speakers during *National Red Ribbon Week* in late October or the *National Public Schools Safety Week* in the spring

See "Armadillo Jim's" www.PutOnYourArmor.org for a list of nationally recognized assemblies, ideas for community outreach and speakers or visit www.schoolshows.com or the *Christian Education Association International* website at www.ceai.org.

A. (See photos on next page of a program related to an assembly in a public school in McAlester, Oklahoma.)

In the following photos, teachers, community leaders and students learn about armadillos and how to *Put On Your Armor*™. *Power Chokes*®, a division of *ExProGroup*® an oilfield service and equipment company with world headquarters in Cypress (Houston), Texas sponsored "Armadillo Jim" and *Put On Your Armor*™. *Power Chokes*® has a district office in the city of McAlester, Oklahoma. Representatives of the company were involved in the school assemblies. Bookmarks bearing the corporate identity were handed to every student. A follow-up crusade featuring "Armadillo Jim" and hosted by the churches in the community was slated for a later date.

B. In 1998 the First Baptist Church of Springdale, Arkansas, headed by Pastor Ronnie Floyd (member of the Southern Baptist Convention) and Children's Pastor, Rev. Dale Hudson, sponsored "Armadillo Jim" into 10 of the area's 20 public elementary schools. During the school assemblies, free tickets were distributed to all students promoting an upcoming community drug-free rally and carnival being held the following Saturday morning. The church's follow-up community rally featured:

- Games
- Carnival
- DARE car
- Sports celebrities

- Rides
- Face Painting
- Elected officials

The attendants of the rally were later invited into the adjacent stadium to receive free door prizes, as a prelude to a crusade and gospel message. At the beginning of this program the city mayors of Springdale and Fayetteville, Arkansas challenged one another in a media event and audience attraction called the *Armadillo Derby*™.

Parents, friends, neighbors and relatives enjoyed a once in a lifetime Billy Graham-type crusade, ala armadillo style. This *Armor Crusade* and school outreach still ranks as one of the most successful community outreaches and events in the *Put On Your Armor*™ foundation's history and "Armadillo Jim's" career. For more information on how you can "armor" your city and schools, contact Jim at www.ArmadilloJim.com or www.PutOnYourArmor.org.

— 22 —
Sponsor a suicide awareness seminar in the school one evening

Offer a free meal or other incentives. Suicide is the number one killer of teenagers after drunk driving.

— 23 —
Sponsor a *Mothers Against Drunk Drivers* (MADD) chapter at your local school or get involved in the *Strides for Change* annual awareness campaign

Go to www.madd.org. There are many speakers, programs, exhibits and demonstrations available for sponsorship. Be sure to contact local law enforcement agencies, other teen outreach organizations, wrecker companies, automobile dealers and alternative beverage companies for co-sponsorship and donations.

— 24 —
Sponsor an abuse awareness seminar in the school one evening

Child and spouse abuse is at epidemic levels in America. Help stop this scourge with this tremendous outreach. Offer outlets for further counseling and safe houses as part of your program.

— 25 —
Sponsor parenting conferences

Donate snacks, food and drinks. Sponsor childcare and a play area for children during this conference enabling anyone to attend. Contact *Focus on the Family* at www.family.org or another great resource, *Family Life Today* at www.familylife.com.

— 26 —
Sponsor bereavement seminars

Grief is the most avoided subject in the American culture, yet emotional pain injures more people annually then any physical pain. Some resources are www.icriedtoo.org and the *Grief Recovery Institute* whose web address is www.grief-recovery.com. Their recommended book is *When Children Grieve*. Other books are *I Cried Too* authored by Jim & Sheila Schmidt, *Life After Death* by Rev. Tony Cooke and *Mourning to Morning* by Rev. Harry and Cheryl Salem (see contact information in the resource section at the back of the book).

Showing you care at a time of grief is one of the greatest gifts you can give someone. Five thousand children a day lose a mom or dad to death, abuse, divorce or imprisonment.

—27—

Sponsor *Honor Roll* awards or the *National Honor Society*

Contact the local school to get involved and be sure to visit the NHS website at www.nhs.us. Businesses in your community may get involved by donating prizes as awards to honorees. You can host *NHS* events at your facility or at the school. You can also partner with the *NHS* in the Prudential Spirit of Community Awards. Visit www.principals.org.

—28—

Participate in Career Day by speaking to students on this annual day in public schools

Ask your members to join you as you put a team of professionals together from your organization or club, or church. Many schools also host Shadow Day where students accompany someone like a parent or other adult to their workplace. Be sure to participate and encourage your members to do the same.

—29—

Sponsor children of prisoners

Adopt them on special weekends and provide necessary provisions such as postage, stationery and envelopes. Take the child's photo, hand or footprints and other special keepsakes and help send these to their imprisoned parent. Become a *Big Brother or Big Sister*. Visit www.bbbs.org.

Participate or become a substitute parent during special events where a parent is needed. Help each child understand that it is okay to love someone (who may be in prison) and not love something they do or did. Remember to host special events like a Christmas party for these children. Host this in the school if appropriate. Please visit Chuck

Colson's *Prison Fellowship Ministry* to learn about *Operation Angle Tree* or other great programs for children of imprisoned parents at: www.pfm.org.

—30—

Sponsor *I Cried Too*® packets for counselors, librarians or classrooms

Visit www.ICriedToo.org. Five thousand children a day lose a mom or dad in America. Many children in local public schools need help to overcome the loss of a parent to death, divorce, abuse or imprisonment. One church member sponsored an *I Cried Too*® children's book to a local public school teacher. As an incentive for his class, the teacher offered a reading area for students who finished their lessons on time. Several students showed marked improvement in classroom behavior and achievement, thus receiving the privilege of reading the *I Cried Too* book in the reward reading area. After several days of reading the book, the students opened up to the teacher and told him how they were dealing with personal loss. One had lost a grandparent, one had lost a dad in a divorce and another was dealing with abuse in the home.

Be sure to ask the principal to inform you of any special days or deaths or other bereavement at the school.

Author's Note: This is one of the most essential healing tools in today's society. I highly recommend doing this one for your school and community. Get the school counselors involved!

—31—

Sponsor a Valentine's Day party and send flowers or chocolate to teachers on Valentine's Day

Check with the room sponsors, parents and nutrition advisors before this project. You may also want to obtain a list of the teacher's birthdays and remember this special day, too with a gift certificate, or special gift.

—32—

Sponsor a Christmas play, Thanksgiving play, Easter play or other holiday appropriate event in the school

—33—

Sponsor kites, goggles, floaties, umbrellas, toys, surfing and swim gear, sports gear, pet collars and Id tags

Order these products with your logo or identification. Offer free kite-flying lessons, swimming lessons, surfing instructions and mentoring on appropriate seasons, sports, hobbies, etc.

—34—

Distribute Bible tracts on property nearest the school

Remember to observe all city and county ordinances regarding distribution of printed material and your freedom of speech.

—35—

Sponsor and care for flower boxes and flowerbeds or water ponds on the school property

What a terrific outlet for the green thumbs and gardeners of your organization. A beautiful atmosphere helps to create a happier feeling for all. Why not consider building a water feature?

—36—

Help develop Patriotism among students:

- Donate *America's God and Country* best selling reference book and CD series by Bill Federer to history teachers, educators, principals, leaders and superintendents. This million seller reference book is a must as it contains quotes, speeches, inaugural addresses and details of events related to our Founding Fathers, the constitution and other historical documents. Visit their website at www.amerisearch.net.

- Forward the *American Minute* daily email to history teachers, superintendents, administrators, school board members and principals. Visit www.amerisearch.net. Recipients of this email will have a daily reminder of something special in history of that day. What a special treat EVERYDAY for a history teacher.

- Invite nationally known speakers such as Bill Federer, David Barton, Peter Marshall, Peter Enns and others to your community to address the students. These men are very knowledgeable of American history and how our schools were founded. You will be very encouraged and motivated after hearing these patriotic speakers. Visit www.amerisearch.net, www.wallbuilders.com, www.petermarshallministries.com, and www.americaspoet.com.

- Donate a new flag to a school. Ask any veteran to help you. Visit www.flags.com.

- Purchase coffee mugs and other gift items personalized with patriotic quotes for history teachers and for display in classrooms. www.amerisearch.net is a great resource for this.

- Donate Lynn Chaney's book, The *ABC's of Patriotism*

- Donate "Armadillo Jim's" upcoming book, *Raising Great Americans; 101 Ways to Increase Patriotism*.

- Sponsor the school librarian or history teacher to the *Reclaiming America* annual conference hosted by best selling author and lecturer, Dr. D. James Kennedy. Pay for their hotel and airline ticket to the annual event held in Florida each year. Visit www.reclaimamerica.org.

- Remember the history teachers during Black History month, Veteran's Day, your state's and city's historical celebrations and other historical times by offering volunteers, expertise or gifts.

- Give scholarships to members wanting to become history teachers in public schools.

- Provide paper and stationery and contact information of local active military so students can write letters to America's uniformed servants. This is always important especially in time of war. Trips to other countries or at sea can be a time of loneliness for many military personnel.

- Provide a list of all the locations where students can find an American flag displayed in your community such as the post office, courthouse, churches and businesses. You can create a contest with this, offering a prize to the student who names the most locations of where flags are displayed in your community or captures the best photos of such.

- Encourage your organization's members to display their flags. Offer prizes to those who submit "best photos"/settings of their flags being flown on their property.

- Help Veterans tell their stories to students. One way to do this is to compile a group of letters into a three-ring binder from veterans in your organization or peer area. These letters can be keepsakes from wars past. Read these historic documents to students in history class or to the entire student assembly on Veteran's Day. Add the veteran's military enlistment photo on a projector screen or displayed at the school. What a great way to honor veterans while encouraging patriotism and appreciation in your students. If your organization has media facilities, capture the audio or video of a veteran and offer it to your school's library, history teachers or speaker's bureau.

— 37 —
Sponsor your band, equipment, props or musicians for the school Christmas musical

Consider renting the school, give tickets away and perform your show there as a holiday event. Sponsor Santa Clause to the school during an evening or after school event where you can also showcase the true Christmas story. Offer printed song and music sheets of traditional Christmas songs and print them: Compliments of "your organization".

— 38 —
Offer your facility or media center for any school event or large audience event like an award ceremony, a play or a high school baccalaureate or graduation ceremony

If you have facilities like media centers offer to record the event. Also, if your facility has production and recording studios or a publications department invite the school's journalism and broadcast classes to visit or use the space and equipment. Internship serve as a great way to expand your reach to students. If you are writing a sermon or speech invite students to edit or critique the material. In producing radio, television or dvd's be sure to invite students to assist or take on a campaign or subject as a class project. Allow students the opportunity to produce their own programs on your equipment. Awarding part-time jobs serves as a wonderful way to reach more students, too.

−39−
Sponsor an Easter egg hunt and bunny costume at the school

Here you can award special eggs containing coupons redeemable at a special location like your church or business. Large coupons and or money or awards can be awarded during a service or meeting where you can deliver a special Easter message.

−40−
Wash the teacher's cars at least twice a year

Ask your members to bring buckets, hoses and soap to join you in the school parking lot. The teachers will find their cars nice and shiny after school. Make it a surprise and keep it a secret between you and the principal. Leave a calling card; "thank you" from the members of *your organization.*

−41−
Sponsor bottled water in the teacher's lounge (add your own label/logo)

—42—

Sponsor summer or anytime reading clubs and Bible clubs at the school

Encourage your members to become reading tutors as school. Contact *Child Evangelism Fellowship* at www.cefonline.com about their *Good News Club* and summer Bible programs. Also remember #3, *Kids for Christ USA* Bible clubs at www.kfcusa.org.

—43—

Host your VBS at the local school

Vacation Bible School is one of the greatest opportunities for summer outreach. By sponsoring this event at the public school, you will offer a neutral sight and you will break down any mental barriers from un-churched parents who may be reluctant to attend a church facility. Also, distribute approved flyers and invitations for your VBS to the schools through the school district office before the end of the school year. Expand this idea by sponsoring a VBS at the facility or campus of your community's largest employer. Imagine the ease for an employee who can just bring their children to work and allow you the opportunity to "teach" them for a day or week! This is what is called a great, "cross promotion".

—44—

Host and sponsor a special speaker and meal at the school twice a year

Many great communicators and speakers often visit communities, corporations and churches. Make sure these trained communicators and speakers maximize their time in your city by speaking to students and teachers at your local schools while they are in town. Many times local civic clubs like the *Kiwanis, Rotary, Lyons, Jaycees, Chamber of Commerce, Optismists, Civitans* and others feature speakers at their events and lunches. Most industries and associations have a speaker's bureau. One such is the energy industry with associations like the *Society of Petroleum Engineers,* www.spe.org, the *American Petroleum Institute,* www.api.org and the *Geology Society* at www.geosociety.org.

Several of these organizations offer student chapters or campus outreaches. The *Oilfield Christian Fellowship* with world headquarters in Houston, Texas and chapters across America sponsors a speaker's bureau and tour to campuses called: *Success & Faith in the Energy Industry* Lecture Series.

You can contact *OCF* from their website at: www.OilfieldChristianFellowship.com.

You can also contact the *National Speakers Association* asking them to help in this endeavor. Their website is www.nsaspeaker.org. You can also contact local chapters of the *Toastmasters International* at www.toastmasters.org.

—45—
Help single moms of students

Sponsor a free (minor) auto repair and clinic on a Saturday morning at the local public school. Give the *Single Mom's Free Car Checkup* tickets away at the school or in the nearby neighborhood. Also, host special sports and clothes "swap days". A church, Braebun Valley Baptist in Houston has a special program called: Alpha

Ministries, a Men's Ministry which caters to the needs of a congregation and the church itself. This program can easily be extended to any local public school. Below are details provided by one of the Alpha Ministries participants, Don Burruto:

> We meet on the first Saturday of each month from 8 a.m. - Noon (or later) We help out the elderly, widows and single mom's with any chores they need help with - moving furniture, fixing a fence, putting up shelves, etc. We also help out around the church and tend to any needs – last month we mulched and planted flowers.

> None of us are full-time handymen, but we are lucky to have an electrician in our group and other men who are happy to do God's work. Together, we usually get the job done.

> We started this in April of 2005 and have anywhere from 6 to 10 guys show up once a month. It is great fellowship time and a lot of fun to get together with the men of the church.

> We put an announcement in the church bulletin the week prior as a reminder to the congregation. We keep our work order forms in a basket in the back of the church, so people with needs can fill out their contact information and the nature of the assistance they need. I call each of those with needs on the Thursday before we get together, along with my reminder calls to the Alphas.

> It has been a real blessing to our church. God always provides what we need! My pastor told me that true religion is tending to widows and orphans.

> I will forward you the form that we use as soon as I can. Who knows, maybe some other churches will start doing this.

—46—
Host a recycling day at the school

Coordinate this with your city and county so they can provide dump trucks and personnel to help with the program. Invite your members to wear special clothes displaying your organization's insignia. Contact recycling associations for ideas on this outreach: www.nrc-recycle.org.

—47—
Host a special "sports garage sale" or "sports swap"

Making it easy for moms (or dads) to upgrade equipment like gloves and cleats for their children, without paying retail. Invite all grade levels to participate making the choice for upgrades in sizes very easy.

—48—
Sponsor *"In God We Trust"* signs in the school

Visit the American Family Association
Website at www.afa.net.

—49—
Sponsor faith-filled book covers such as the Ten Commandments

Offer other great children's promotional items like: backpacks, coin purses, mouse pads, stickers, rain gear, lunch boxes, paper sack lunch bags, rulers, note pads, pencils, playing cards and others. You can private label these as well as juice and water bottles too. Safety whistles, cell phone covers and other high tech items are available.

Visit www.childrensministry.com. Sponsor special T-shirts and other faith apparel. Visit the *I Believe®* campaign for one such example at www.ibelievethemovement.com.

— 50 —

Sponsor numerous sports/physical fitness-related events like:

- Honor the scholastic athletes of the year. You can combine this with their annual awards ceremony letting them know that their community is proud of them too.

- Host a sports banquet featuring a famous guest speaker. Many pro players will be delighted to come to your event to make a difference in the life of a child.

- Sponsor coaches into a local golf tournament like the PK, *In His Grip* golf tournament. Visit www.inhisgripgolf.com.

- Train and provide referees, judges and umpires for all sports. Provide rule books with your insignia on the cover. For more information you can visit this web site www.everyrule.com/sports_az_list.html.

- Open your church or your facility for pre-game meals, team meetings and media events or parent booster club gatherings. In Yukon, Oklahoma five churches rotate the sponsorship and preparation of the football team's pre-home-game meals.

Include a motivational speaker and keepsake of this annual event.

- Sponsor local, regional and state events like bike-a-thons, marathons, *March of Dimes Walks, Breast Cancer Awareness Month* and other nationally recognized annual health campaigns.

- Contact *Fellowship of Christian Athletes* to see what programs they are already doing in local schools and partner with them. See *FCA* chapter contacts at www.FCA.org. Also visit the *Champions for Christ* website at www.championsfc.com.

- Sponsor and host the *Punt, Pass & Kick*® competition at a local school. See www.nflyouthfootball.com.

- Find special events associated with all sports like swimming, soccer, softball, surfing, rodeo, golf, tennis, hockey, baseball and all others. Visit the websites of all the above for more ideas and sponsorship opportunities on a local level.

- Visit the *President's Council on Physical Fitness* to partner with them in schools in various outreaches: visit: www.fitness.gov.

- Sponsor camps and other athletic activities. Contact partners such as Coca-cola maker of Dasani to assist in your outreach for healthy choices: Visit: www.cokecce.com.

Coordinate activities related to sports and fitness with the *American Alliance for Health, Physical Education, Recreation and Dance.* www.aahperd.org.

AAHPERD is made up of five nonprofit associations with over 30,000 members nationwide. The organizations are:

    a. AAPAR — *American Association for Physical Activity and Recreation*
    b. AAHE — *American Association for Health Education*
    c. NAGWS — *National Association for Girls and Women in Sport*
    d NASPE — *National Association for Sport and Physical Education*
    e NDA — *National Dance Association*

The goal of AAHPERD is to promote quality physical and health education, including educating students about the health benefits of being physically active, eating right and living tobacco-free.

AAPHERD programs and award ceremonies related to *Hoops for the Heart*™ and *Jump Rope for the Heart*™ can be hosted at your facility. You can also visit the *American Heart Association* at their website, www.americanheart.org for more ideas about other events related to health and physical education.

- You can also sponsor local, regional and state events like bike-a-thons, marathons, *March of Dimes Walks, Breast Cancer Awareness Month* and other nationally recognized annual health campaigns. Other activities and events related to sports and health are the *Diabetes Foundation's School Walk*. Information can be found at http://schoolwalk.diabetes.org or www.diabetes.org. You can host the *Tour de Cure* bike ride at your facility or involve your members as volunteers. Promote this at the local schools and giveaway bikes and other prizes at your event. Visit www.tour.diabetes.org. Further information and programs related to diabetes can be found at: www.diabetes.org/support-the-cause/community-campaign.jsp.

- Be sure to encourage your organization to be involved in the *Juvenile Diabetes Research Foundation* and all of their local school and youth events. Find information at: www.jdrf.org.

- Join the *American Cancer Society* annual *Relay for Life*. Your facility is the perfect place for hosting such event. Visit www.cancer.org for all their information.

- The *March of Dimes* conducts an annual walk and always looks for partnerships. Visit www.marchofdimes.com.

- MDA or the *Muscular Dystrophy Association* has a variety of athletic and physical events associated with its organization such as:

  > Bowling Against Dystrophy
  > Golf
  > The Great Walk®
  > Hop-a-Thon®
  > Lock-Up
  > Shamrocks Against Dystrophy®
  > Youth Programs
  > Special Events

- Many children like to fish. Advertise a fishing tournament in the school and giveaway the prizes one evening at the school. You can also find other fishing events online and by visiting the *Kids All American Fishing* sponsored by *Wal*Mart* at www.kids-fishing.com.

Depending on your area of the country there are numerous sports and physical activities related to specific geographic conditions like snowboarding, surfing, ice skating, hunting, soccer and many more. Google® the web for great ideas on how you can promote these activities and create special events in your public schools.

Remember to plan and work with the school's physical education instructors and coaches while endeavoring your events. You can legally place posters in the schools about such events provided you receive the permission from an authorizing person.

—51—
Honor musicians of the year from local schools

Nominate musicians for scholarships and give award winners the opportunity to perform in your special event, venue or seasonal celebrations. Feature any of them as the "opening act" at some of your community events. The *Grammy® Foundation* and the *Dove Awards®* programs offer membership and may offer scholarship opportunities. Obtain promotional tickets and award them or use them as incentives for any contest or event you sponsor in the school. For *Grammy®* information visit www.grammy.com.

To learn more about the *Dove Awards®* and their partnership programs visit the *Gospel Music Association* website at www.gmamusicawards.com. Remember to co-sponsor and work with the manufacturers and retailers of musical instruments. Many of these manufacturers host their own awards programs and incentives. You may be able to garner a grand prize from one of these national companies provided you have a good promotional/advertising and business plan. Visit the websites of companies who market musical instruments to children and youth to learn more and obtain innovative ideas. You can work with a local radio station.

—52—
Host scholastic and other events on the local level like the National Spelling Bee, Geography Bee, Bible Challenge, Math Challenge and Essay Contests

—53—
Honor a Family of the Year

The international organization, *Focus on the Family* with Dr. James Dobson or *Family Life Today* offers many ideas and ways to promote the family in your community or public school. websites: www.family.org or www.familylife.org.

Many local businesses will donate prizes gift certificates, gift basket and other items for this family. Sponsor a family photo contest with such awards as a free meal at a popular restaurant, a camping trip or equipment or new tableware. A grand prize could be a family retreat or vacation. There are many theme parks and hotels who will be interested in co-sponsoring this with you in your community and schools. Students can win this grand prize from an incentive drawing based on attendance, the family photo or essay contest, improved grades, behavioral improvement or a community project. Involve teachers or a committee comprised of members of your community in the selection process.

—54—
Honor a student's Community Project of the Year

At the beginning of each year send press releases and announcements about your *School Community Project of the Year* campaign. Outline the criteria and list examples like the one below. Present a scholarship, large cash award and special recognition. Involve the mayor, other civic leaders, club presidents and members of the media by asking them to judge or nominate projects.

Community School Project of the Year
(Example)

This past November, Kelly Smith of Ridgeway Jr. High accompanied her friend, Shelly Jones to her dental appointment. While in the waiting room of the clinic which is located on the north side of our city and in an area where Kelly does not live or frequently visit, she noticed there were only a few books for children to read, especially books for younger children. The next day, after Kelly suggested to her teacher that her class collect books and deliver them

Certificate of Merit
This certificate is awarded to

Kelly Smith School Community Project of the Year Winner

Signatures   Date

to the clinic, which by the way is on the lower-income side of town, her principal, Samantha Jerrel, invited Kelly to make the project an all school project. Kelly used the school microphone and announcement time each morning encouraging her classmates and schoolmates to bring books for the clinics on the north side. After one week, more than 400 "almost new" books were collected. Other clinics on the north side heard about the program and requested the resources, too. The campaign was extended and consequently expanded to the other two Jr. Highs;

William McKinley and George Washington Carver. Nearly 1600 "almost new" books, puzzles and coloring books were collected. Altogether these items provided resources for 26 clinics and doctors' offices on the city's north side. I nominate Kelly for your Community Project of the Year.

The national Make A Difference Day celebrated each fourth Saturday of October is a perfect cosponsor for any of your special projects. Visit www.makeadifferenceday.com and www.pointsoflight.org.

You can also participate in the *National Honor Society and National Association* of *Secondary School Principals award* and their partnership in the *Prudential Spirit of Community Awards*. Visit http://www.principals.org.

**—55—
Host a sex abstinence program or purity seminar for young girls and boys**

The *Oklahoma Family Policy Council's* program called *Kids Eagerly Endorsing Purity* (K.E.E.P) has found tremendous success in the public schools. These conferences will instill lasting values and relationships while encouraging boys and girls to abstain from sex. Sponsor keepsake rings, mementos and certificates. As a follow-up, promote a special night and encourage dads to date their daughters and/or moms to date their sons. Decorate your facility in a special way and offer a special 5-star banquet and celebrity guest speaker.

Also see www.daughtersofheaven.org for more information on a wonderful purity conference for young ladies.

Author's Note: Look for "Armadillo Jim's" upcoming book: *Date your Daughter: 101 Ideas for Your Date Night.*

−56−

Sponsor a licensed and insured petting zoo or a trip to the zoo or local fair or creation seminar display

Give tickets away as prizes or incentives to the school. There are many professional animal handlers and docents who are ready to visit a school. Visit the *International Association of Fairs and Expositions* website at www.fairsandexpos.com or the *USDA Animal Welfare* website for a list of licensed agents, animal handlers, animal edutainment or exhibitors at www.aphis.usda.gov/ac/publications.html. Sponsor books about creation or Noah's Ark to give away as prizes. You can also host the Noah's Ark stage production into your schools and city. Visit www.noahtickets.com. Also available is the Creation Evidence Exhibit and information hosted by well known scientist, Dr. Karl Baugh. Visit www.creationevidence.org.

−57−

Sponsor events related to *Homeland Security* and *National Preparedness Month* in September or *America's Safe Schools Week* or back to school events.

Create stickers, identification tags, signage and 9-1-1 reminders. Provide florescent striping for children's clothes or paint school crosswalks and giveaway bicycle reflectors and other reflective material or stickers with your logo. It's good to help students feel safe. There are many companies who sponsor safety fairs and seminars. Partner with these when appropriate. Visit the websites at www.dhs.gov and www.schoolsafety.us.

—58—

Donate or make your bus and other commercial and insured vehicles available for important school field trips

More importantly, become a school bus driver working full-time or as a substitute driver morning and afternoons, for the school district.

—59—

Sponsor nutrition programs, nutritional snacks after school and/or exercise programs

Some schools have special daycare or events after school where you can supply a nutritional snack. Offer advice and seminars to parents. Visit the *National School Nutrition Association*'s website to learn more at www.schoolnutrition.org.

Organize after school clubs and recruit and train the leadership for these programs. Always certify your volunteers through the *Department of Human Services.*

—60—

Facilitate regional Critical Incident Stress Management (CISM) training

Invite community leaders, teachers, police and fire departments, EMS staff, floor wardens, other pastors, custodians and bus drivers. Host this event in a school.

Melissa Slagle, renowned CISM trainer will visit your community to conduct this 10-hour training. Melissa can be contacted at *Living Solutions* at livingsolutions@sbcglobal.net

Critical Incident Stress Management's website is www.CISM.org. Please read Melissa Slagle's book: *The Church's Response Following A Disaster*, paying special attention to "Armadillo Jim's" chapter: *The Church's Response to Children Following A Disaster: 101 Ways to help your children find the road to recovery.*

—61—
Sponsor graduation gifts to selected recipients and participate in Project Graduation

Also, sponsor your photographer for special senior pictures. Display these in your community in such places as grocery stores, business lobbies, church lobbies and hallways of frequently visited public facilities. Place your logo on these photos with a Bible verse such as Jeremiah 29:11 or add a positive note of congratulations on the photo frame. Make this your annual event.

—62—
Hold a service or special event once a year in a local school

This will give your congregation or business associates a vision for local schools by seeing what the facility is like. Many in your organization have not set foot in a school since graduating from high school.

—63—
Donate appropriate books/videos DVDs and CDs to the school library and aftercare clubs

(See "Armadillo Jim's" upcoming book *101 Best Books and DVDs for children, ie: Little House on the Prairie, Veggie Tales*).

—64—

Sponsor the school website and/or link your website to provide vital and timely local school information

Offer information such as school closings, bus routes, school calendar, menu, sports schedules, holidays, PTA meetings, event schedules and more.

—65—

Provide and train volunteers, senior citizens and retired executives as mentors

They can help students learn such things as banking, balancing a checkbook and starting a small business like lawn mowing, photography and other services. See www.score.org.

—66—

Sponsor free eye exams and glasses

Offer this to students of singles moms or low income families. *The Lions Club* has excellent resources for this. Remember to contact your local eye doctors for donations. Visit *The Lions Club* at www.lionsclubs.org.

—67—

Provide free tickets to faith-filled events in your community

For example, movie premiers, concerts, speakers, plays, fundraisers, promotions and special events. Many times fairs, waterparks and other attractions in your community will donate tickets which you can use to promote their event and award as prizes to schools.

— 68 —

Sponsor dental products like tooth brushes (add your logo or name) or free dental screening clinics on school property

Recruit professionals within your membership or organization. Some dentists or hygienists may donate their time or help by giving out discount coupons for future office visits or in exchange for advertising in your publications.

— 69 —

Sponsor a health fair and offer free medical supplies

Contact your local doctors, nurses, pediatricians, *Red Cross* and health agencies for product donations and staffing. Make sure to give all volunteers and sponsors credit in advertisements. Always send "thank you" notes.

— 70 —

Recruit other businesses and other churches to partner with you

It is easier to work in unity than to be a lone ranger. Building relationships with the school, along with others in the community will ensure success.

— 71 —

Enjoy lunch with the students

Enjoy special one-on-one days on a very regular basis. Sign up as a mentor through the front office at school or ask your student friend to get permission for your visits.

—72—
Sponsor a faith-based concert and speakers into a public school

Contact www.gospelartists.com or your local radio station and concert promoters for the best deals and contacts.

—73—
Sponsor or purchase lunch boxes or backpacks for needy students

This is a good place to post positive messages, scripture and id/logo.

—74—
Sponsor bikes to needy children who have no transportation

—75—
Sponsor car air-fresheners, sun visors, reflectors, key chains, license plate holders, etc. for newly licensed student drivers

Offer your parking lot to drivers education instructors as an offsite place to practice parallel parking. Host a contest or offer rewards related to safety and good driving records for new drivers, seniors, accident-free drivers, alcohol-free students and others. Offer sponsorship of personalized license plates to the winners.

—76—
Sponsor driver's education and locations

Encourage your youth or children's pastor or your community outreach director to become drivers education instructors. Spending time in a car with a student builds great relationships. Also sponsor CDL training for members who are willing to become bus drivers.

—77—
Sponsor holiday arts and crafts/volunteers

You can also donate decorative items for the school foyer, bathrooms, walls, lounge, offices and other areas. Items could include flower arrangements, plants, pictures and encourage your members to volunteer at the school during special holidays.

—78—
Sponsor school event photos and the photographer. Add your corporate id/logo to each photo

For instance your photographer can attend the next school play, ceremony or sports event. Take photos and then provide a copy of each with your logo on the bottom of the left or right corner along with the name of the event and date. This is a great keepsake of an event. Remember to make the photos in a frame-able size.

—79—
Sponsor a "Student of the Week" or "Athlete of the Week" award in partnership with the local paper

Purchase advertising space in a specific location announcing the winner each week/month. Sponsor a weekly photo and story of a student who has displayed exemplary excellence in community projects or sports that enhanced the school, community, or team. This may be part of your Community Project of the Year program as seen in # 56.

—80—
Donate cash or local retailer gift cards as excellent perks

This is wonderful for teachers and other public school personnel who may have a sudden need. Be sure to offer help or service during a time of crisis, death or loss.

—81—
Become a bus stop guardian or friend

Students often gather at neighborhood street corners, bus stops and designated areas before school. Many of these students are not chaperoned. What a great time for some early risers and retired members or the senior members of your congregation to chaperone these students. Bring fruit, juice, or muffins to these students and share a daily devotion or distribute reading material, such as tracts or Bibles. Be consistent. Contact the local *Department of Human Services* to get proper background checks and credentials for your volunteers.

—82—
Facilitate an after school athletic league or clubs like chess, checkers, bad gammon, etc.

Many home-schoolers need to mix with public school children to help develop social skills. Bringing these two groups together will help create goodwill between the public school and the local home schoolers at a neutral facility like your place.

—83—
Train your senior citizen members of your organization to become mentors before or after school

They can teach various character traits, manners, skills or ethics. What senior citizen would not like to teach some boys or girls how to tie a knot or scale a fish, play tennis, swing a golf club, crochet, sew or other talent? Find sponsors for these programs such as local sporting goods stores, bait shops, hobby stores or whatever applies to the program. Contact local *Department of Human Services* to get proper background checks and credentials for your volunteers.

—84—
Provide special holiday costumed characters for the school

Train your volunteers to create, sew, adorn and then perform in these costumes.

—85—
Sponsor new playground and sporting goods equipment or build a jogging trail

Build this adjacent to the school property. Add your name or logo to the products or play area.

—86—
Sponsor the senior prom or Project Graduation or both

The school district in Yukon, Oklahoma has a tremendous record for parental, community and business involvement for their Project Graduation. Parents who want to chaperone or volunteer during the PG event night must first earn the privilege by soliciting a minimum amount of cash donations and prizes from local businesses. In a recent PG, every graduating senior who attended received an Ipod. Project Gradation is one of the best alcohol-free alternative parties in the nation. The event also fights hunger and illiteracy. Offer your facility as the place to hold the Project Graduation party. For more information visit www.projectgraduation.org. Do the same for the prom, offering your location or a pre-prom, five-star meal at your venue.

—87—
Send a clown, juggler, magician or other entertainer to the school or teacher's lounge

Surprise the students and teachers during their lunch hour. Ask the school to allow you to host a clown or party for the class with the best participation and attendance each week, quarter or school year, depending on your budget and the school's permission.

—88—
Provide your church or business grounds, facilities or parking lot for extra curricular activities

Provide fun activities like skating, tournaments, dirt bike rides, demonstrations, sports practice, club meetings and other events like car shows, tractor pulls, agricultural events or winter wonderlands. Students often need a place to hang out on Friday nights so why not consider outdoor movies, bonfires, coffee houses, or other attractions at your facility? Offer after game events or what some in football call: The Fifth Quarter. Provide a safe haven for such events like surfboard waxing, car displays, cruising stops and as another cultural hangout alternative. Open a coffee house giving away drink coupons in the schools.

−89−

Provide a limousine for the valedictorian, teacher of the year, principal of the year, custodian of the year, or another outstanding public school representative

Schedule the limousine to pick up the recipient at the school to take to a nearby restaurant. Remember to contact the media for a photo op if they have not already been recognized in the local paper and/or news. Remember to include this as one of your awards in your Community Project of the Year campaign as seen in # 58.

−90−

Collect receipts and coupons from your members who purchase at partner retailers who donate a % back to your organization or school

Use these special funds to help in projects for your special public school. Advertise this in your various in-house publications and on your website. Campbell's Soup® and many other food companies offer box top and coupon rebates to local schools. Check with the principals to partner in these financially rewarding programs. *Box Tops for Education* is a wonderful program in which your members can participate and help local schools financially. Learn how your members and organization can get involved at: www.boxtops4education.com.

−91−

Petition your congressman and other elected officials for higher teacher pay, reform in spending allocations and streamlining bureaucracy

This would allow more tax money to go directly to the classroom and classroom teachers.

−92−

Sponsor a meal each week/month/quarter depending on your budget so the cafeteria staff can take a day off

The students will enjoy a change of pace. Include a printed message, devotional or coupons in the lunch bags or meals. Remember to promote nutrition at all times. Celebrate National School Lunch Week sponsored by the *National School Nutrition Association*. You'll need to educate yourself about qualified "Type A" lunch programs. Get some ideas from their website at: www.schoolnutrition.org.

−93−

Sponsor take home products such as food items or products made or marketed by members of your congregation or organization

For instance, if a member has a business making salsa, honey, or pies, purchase these and deliver them to the school as teacher or staff surprise gifts. Add your logo and 'thank you' sticker to the items. Everyone likes a gift, especially when it is homemade.

−94−

Sponsor a parents night out

Offer special nights where parents of public school children can drop off their kids and go out on a date as you "baby sit". Offer discount certificates to movies, dance lessons or restaurants to these parents. After their wonderful night promote an upcoming marriage retreat with a take home flyer or promotional reminder gift.

—95—

Sponsor a marriage retreat for teachers, coaches, parents and staff

A happy educator makes a happy learning environment. Offer child care, free tickets and special door prizes to all attendees. Distribute the invitations and tickets to the local pubic schools and put them on windshields following a sporting event, PTA meeting or another occasion. Ask for special permission to send tickets home through the students. Offer follow-up programs such as marriage renewals or communication and personality difference courses at your facility.

The famous *Laugh Your Way to a Happy Marriage* weekend encounter is one great program for any couple. Visit www.laughyourway.com. Another marriage retreat is sponsored by Dr. Gary and Dr. Greg Smalley through the *Smalley Relationship Center*. The weekend encounter called, *I Promise* helps couples find the DNA of their marriage. Many valuable resources about marriage are also available. Visit www.dnaofrelationships.com. with Dr. Gary Smalley and *Family Life* with Dennis and Barbara Rainey offers *A Weekend to Remember* for couples. Visit www.familylife.com.

—96—

Organize a seminar or assembly about fishing, surfing, ballroom dancing, (or other specialty)

Ask the experts in your church or business to use all their contacts to recruit a professional to visit your community. Then host this professional and their presentation at the school one evening. Plan special promotions like a giveaway or grand prize to a family or father-son, father-daughter, mother-son, mother-daughter team to "go with the pro". Solicit donations for related equipment or apparel to be given away as door prizes, too. Also, you can promote this by erecting a temporary display in front of your church. Examples include a surfboard for a visiting surfer or a canoe or boat for a visiting professional fisherman. Many professionals can be found by visiting a specific association's website.

— 97 —
Learn as much as you can about your local schools and national school statistics

Visit the *Standard and Poors'* website at www.schoolmatters.com or the *National Center for Education Statistics* at www.nces.ed.gov.

— 98 —
Host a New Year's Eve Party at the school

Invite all the students, parents, faculty and staff. Encourage your members to run the games, music, parking, band and refreshments. This event makes a safe alternative for the community. Contact major watch manufacturers for grand prize drawings and other "Father Time" products to help in making the event exciting. This would be a very good opportunity to give-away New Year's calendars emblazoned with your corporate identification.

— 99 —
Host a skating party in your gym, sidewalks or parking lot

Remember that floor hockey and outdoor basket-ball, handball and other sports are conducive to concrete venues.

— 100 —
**Remember to host and sponsor special Christmas events
and promotions in your local schools**

The celebration of the birth of the Savior, Jesus
Christ is the good news everyone likes to hear. This is a
perfect time and reason to share your faith. It is not happy
holidays, it is Merry Christmas.

Some of the ways to share Jesus' birthday are:

- Send Christmas cards to the students and faculty of
  your local public schools.

- Join *Toys for Tots* and other national organizations
  to ensure that all students and children receive at
  least one Christmas present.

- Join the national Christmas campaign, *Angel Tree.*

- Encourage your choir director or members to go
  caroling to the school.

- Donate any type of Christmas gift to the school,
  teachers and students. If your organization or a
  special member has a Christmas CD, donate it.

- Make popcorn balls, candy apples, fruit baskets,
  Christmas cookies and other baked goods for the
  students.

- Deliver a special Christmas ornament to the principal, teachers and / or students. Package these
  items with special wrapping, showcasing your

logo and including a greeting card, message or invitation to a function at your venue.

- Organize a hay ride, meeting at the school and concluding with caroling, homemade wassail, apple cider, hot chocolate and other refreshments.

- Contract Santa Clause to visit the local schools on your behalf.

- Purchase or grow a Christmas tree for the local school and deliver it fully decorated a few weeks before Christmas. Let your children's department and other groups place special ornaments and messages on the tree.

- Remember to include your corporate identification and other information on all items and packaging related to the above. Encourage your ladies' and men's clubs, Sunday school classes, youth groups and others to join in the preparation and projects. Try to advertise the events and join in partnership with local radio and television stations. Expand your market by thinking outside the box and work with local retailers and all members of your community.

—101—

Pray again

Ask God for new ideas to bless your public school and then DO SOMETHING, ANYTHING. Sometimes just an appreciation note goes a long way.

Remember that creating good will and forming strong relationships with your local educators, civic leaders, businessmen and women, other pastors and families will open more doors and opportunities for you. If at least one teacher, principal, coach, educator, custodian, bus driver or staff member from a local public school is not a recipient of one of your Christmas cards, it's time to get to work.

Always show appreciation and you will win the favor of your local school officials and educators. This will enable you to increase your influence and significance while reaching more students in helping public schools.

Author's Note: I believe you will choose to make a difference in public schools. As a step of faith I have recently registered the website www.PublicSchoolChaplains.org

I believe that one day soon, millions more students will hear the good news of Jesus Christ in public schools. Chaplains will be allowed to freely walk the hallways and minister to the tremendous needs of students on a day to day basis.

When you walk by faith and not by sight, God is pleased. Let's work together to please God while blessing our public schools.

I'll be praying for you!

Big Suggestions

You will find an excellent example of bridging the gap done by the Assemblies of God through their Character Connex public school program. This character educational assembly program is a tool for developing great relationships with school administrators and educators while at the same time fulfilling the public school's need for training their students. Visit www.characterconnex.com, www.4kids.ag.org, www.afterschoolmentoring.org for *KidsCare®* and *Youth Alive* campus outreach ideas at www.yausa.com.

Be sure to enter into partnerships with campus organizations such as:

1. *Campus Crusade for Christ;* www.ccci.org
2. *Youth for Christ;* www.yfc.org
3. *YoungLife;* www.younglife.org
4. *ChiAlpha Ministries;* www.chialpha.com
5. *Fellowship of Christian Athletes;* www.fca.org
6. *Champions for Christ;* www.championsfc.com

There are many other programs available which have been successfully implemented by churches, civic organizations and religious organizations. You would do well to search the web to find and then contact the denominations and organizations that have already been involved in public schools. Do some interviewing of the directors of these programs before you get started. Remember that there is a tremendous blessing when brethren dwell together in unity. Psalm 133. Don't reinvent the wheel. Do some homework. Leaders of other successful programs are always happy to share their vision and experiences.

Also get involved with the *International Exchange Student* program headed by the *Rotary International*. Host an international exchange student in your home and sponsor a special *International Exchange Student* banquet or event at your facility. Contact www.rotary.org or other groups such as www.ayusa.org. Search the web for more exchange student programs.

Hollywood filmmaker, George Lucas' foundation, Edutopia has some very interesting information and learning opportunities. visit www.edutopia.org.

APPENDIX 1

(20 U.S.C. §§ 4071-74)
DENIAL OF EQUAL ACCESS PROHIBITED

Sec. 4071. (a) It shall be unlawful for any public secondary school which receives Federal financial assistance and which has a limited open forum to deny equal access or a fair opportunity to, or discriminate against, any students who wish to conduct a meeting within that limited open forum on the basis of the religious, political, philosophical, or other content of the speech at such meetings.

(b) A public secondary school has a limited open forum whenever such school grants an offering to or opportunity for one or more non-curriculum related student groups to meet on school premises during non-instructional time.

(c) School shall be deemed to offer a fair opportunity to students who wish to conduct a meeting within its limited open forum if such school uniformly provides that-the meeting is voluntary and student-initiated; there is no sponsorship of the meeting by the school, the government, or its agents or employees; employees or agents of the school or government are present at religious meetings only in a non-participatory capacity; the meeting does not materially and substantially interfere with the orderly conduct of educational activities within he school; and non-school persons may not direct, conduct, control, or regularly attend activities of student groups.

(d) Nothing in this subchapter shall be construed to authorize the United States or any state or political subdivision thereof-to influence the form or content of any prayer or other religious activity; to require any person to participate in prayer or other religious activity; to expend public funds beyond the incidental cost of providing the space for student-initiated meetings; to compel any school agent or employee to attend a school meeting if the content of the speech at the meeting is contrary to the beliefs of the agent or employee; to sanction meetings that are otherwise unlawful; to limit the rights of groups of students which are not of a specified numerical size; or to abridge the constitutional rights of any person.

(e) Not withstanding the availability of any other remedy under the Constitution or the laws of the United States, nothing in this subchapter shall be construed to authorize the United States to deny or withhold Federal financial assistance to any school.

(f) Nothing in this subchapter shall be construed to limit the authority of the school, its agents or employees, to maintain order and discipline on school premises, to protect the well-being of students and faculty and to assure that attendance of students at meetings is voluntary.

DEFINITIONS

Sec. 4072. As used in this subchapter-

The term "secondary school" means a public school which provides secondary education as determined by State law.

The term "sponsorship" includes the act of promoting, leading, or participating in a meeting. The assignment of a teacher, administrator, or other school employee to a meeting for custodial purposes does not constitute sponsorship of the meeting.

The term "meeting" includes those activities of student groups which are permitted under a school's limited open forum and are not directly related to the school curriculum.

The term "non-instructional time" means time set aside by the school before actual classroom instruction begins or after actual classroom instruction ends.

SEVERABILITY

Sec. 4073. If any provision of this subchapter or the application thereof to any person or circumstances is judicially determined to be invalid, the provisions of the remainder of the subchapter and the application to other persons or circumstances shall not be affected thereby.

CONSTRUCTION

Sec. 4074. The provisions of this subchapter shall supersede all other provisions of Federal law that are inconsistent with the provisions of this subchapter.

You should also be familiar with the Department of Education Guidelines, www.ed.gov/policy/gen/guid/religionand-schools/prayer_guidance.html which state:

"Students may organize prayer groups, religious clubs and 'see you at the pole' gatherings before school to the same extent that students are permitted to organize other non-curricular student activity groups. Such groups must be given the same access to the school facilities for assembling as is given to other non-curricular groups."

Thankfully you can find all of this information in an easy-to-read and newly updated guide called *Teachers Religion in Public Schools*. It is produced by the Center for Law and Religious Freedom of the Christian Legal Society www.clsnet.org and the Christian Educators Association International; www.ceai.org .The guide uses three easy symbols — a green light, a stop sign and a warning signal — to indicate whether a particular practice is legally permissible today in the public schools. I want to strongly encourage you to get this great resource into your hands and into the hands of teachers, administrators, other parents, or students connected with the public schools.

Guidance on Constitutionally Protected Prayer in Public Elementary and Secondary Schools

February 7, 2003

INTRODUCTION

Section 9524 of the Elementary and Secondary Education Act ("ESEA") of 1965, as amended by the No Child Left Behind Act of 2001, requires the Secretary to issue guidance on constitutionally protected prayer in public elementary and secondary schools. In addition, Section 9524 requires that, as a condition of receiving ESEA funds, a local educational agency ("LEA") must certify in writing to its State educational agency ("SEA") that it has no policy that prevents, or otherwise denies participation in, constitutionally protected prayer in public schools as set forth in this guidance.

The purpose of this guidance is to provide SEAs, LEAs and the public with information on the current state of the law concerning constitutionally protected prayer in the public schools and thus to clarify the extent to which prayer in public schools is legally protected. This guidance also sets forth the responsibilities of SEAs and LEAs with respect to Section 9524 of the ESEA. As required by the Act, this guidance has been jointly approved by the Office of the General Counsel in the Department of Education and the Office of Legal Counsel in the Department of Justice as reflecting the current state of the law. It will be made available on the Internet through the Department of Education's web site (www.ed.gov). The guidance will be updated on a biennial basis, beginning in September 2004, and provided to SEAs, LEAs, and the public.

THE SECTION 9524 CERTIFICATION PROCESS

In order to receive funds under the ESEA, an LEA must certify in writing to its SEA that no policy of the LEA prevents, or otherwise denies participation in, constitutionally protected prayer in public elementary and secondary schools as set forth in this guidance. An LEA must provide this certification to the SEA by October 1, 2002, and by October 1 of each subsequent year during which the LEA participates in an ESEA program. However, as a transitional matter, given the timing of this guidance, the initial certification must be provided by an LEA to the SEA by March 15, 2003.

The SEA should establish a process by which LEAs may provide the necessary certification. There is no specific Federal form that an LEA must use in providing this certification to its SEA. The certification may be provided as part of the application process for ESEA programs, or separately and in whatever form the SEA finds most appropriate, as long as the certification is in writing and clearly states that the LEA has no policy that prevents, or otherwise denies participation in, constitutionally protected prayer in public elementary and secondary schools as set forth in this guidance.

By November 1 of each year, starting in 2002, the SEA must send to the Secretary a list of those LEAs that have not filed the required certification or against which complaints have been made to the SEA that the LEA is not in compliance with this guidance. However, as a transitional matter, given the timing of this guidance, the list otherwise due November 1, 2002, must be sent to the Secretary by April 15, 2003. This list should be sent to:

Office of Elementary and Secondary Education
Attention: Jeanette Lim
U.S. Department of Education
400 Maryland Avenue, S.W.
Washington, D.C. 20202

The SEA's submission should describe what investigation or enforcement action the SEA has initiated with respect to each listed LEA and the status of the investigation or action. The SEA should not send the LEA certifications to the Secretary, but should maintain these records in accordance with its usual records retention policy.

ENFORCEMENT OF SECTION 9524

LEAs are required to file the certification as a condition of receiving funds under the ESEA. If an LEA fails to file the required certification, or files it in bad faith, the SEA should ensure compliance in accordance with its regular enforcement procedures. The Secretary considers an LEA to have filed a certification in bad faith if the LEA files the certification even though it has a policy that prevents, or otherwise denies participation in, constitutionally protected prayer in public elementary and secondary schools as set forth in this guidance.

The General Education Provisions Act ("GEPA") authorizes the Secretary to bring enforcement actions against recipients of Federal education funds that are not in compliance with the law. Such measures may include withholding funds until the recipient comes into compliance. Section 9524 provides the Secretary with specific authority to issue and enforce orders with respect to an LEA that fails to provide the required certification to its SEA or files the certification in bad faith.

OVERVIEW OF GOVERNING CONSTITUTIONAL PRINCIPLES

The relationship between religion and government in the United States is governed by the First Amendment to the Constitution, which both prevents the government from establishing religion and protects privately initiated religious expression and activities from government interference and discrimination. [1] The First Amendment thus establishes certain limits on the conduct of public school officials as it relates to religious activity, including prayer.

The legal rules that govern the issue of constitutionally protected prayer in the public schools are similar to those that govern religious expression generally. Thus, in discussing the operation of Section 9524 of the ESEA, this guidance sometimes speaks in terms of "religious expression." There are a variety of issues relating to religion in the public schools, however, that this guidance is not intended to address.

The Supreme Court has repeatedly held that the First Amendment requires public school officials to be neutral in their treatment of religion, showing neither favoritism toward nor hostility against religious expression such as prayer. [2] Accordingly, the First Amendment forbids religious activity that is sponsored by the government but protects religious activity that is initiated by private individuals, and the line between government-sponsored and privately initiated religious expression is vital to a proper understanding of the First Amendment's scope. As the Court has explained in several cases, "there is a crucial difference between *government* speech endorsing religion, which the Establishment Clause forbids, and *private* speech endorsing religion, which the Free Speech and Free Exercise Clauses protect." [3]

The Supreme Court's decisions over the past forty years set forth principles that distinguish impermissible governmental religious speech from the constitutionally protected private religious speech of students. For example, teachers and other public school officials may not lead their classes in prayer, devotional readings from the Bible, or other religious activities. [4] Nor may school officials attempt to persuade or compel students to participate in prayer or other religious activities. [5] Such conduct is "attributable to the State" and thus violates the Establishment Clause. [6]

Similarly, public school officials may not themselves decide that prayer should be included in school-sponsored events. In *Lee v. Weisman* [7], for example, the Supreme Court held that public school officials violated the Constitution in inviting a member of the clergy to deliver a prayer at a graduation ceremony. Nor may school officials grant religious speakers preferential access to public audiences, or otherwise select public speakers on a basis that favors religious speech. In *Santa Fe Independent School District v. Doe* [8], for example, the Court invalidated a school's football game speaker policy on the ground that it was designed by school officials to result in pregame prayer, thus favoring religious expression over secular expression.

Although the Constitution forbids public school officials from directing or favoring prayer, students do not "shed their constitutional rights to freedom of speech or expression at the schoolhouse gate," [9] and the Supreme Court has made clear that "private religious speech, far from being a First Amendment orphan, is as fully protected under the Free Speech Clause as secular private expression." [10] Moreover, not all religious speech that takes place in the public schools or at school-sponsored events is governmental speech. [11] For example, "nothing in the Constitution ... prohibits any public school student from voluntarily praying at any time before, during, or after the school day," [12] and students may pray with fellow students during the school day on the same terms and conditions that they may engage in other conversation or speech. Likewise, local school authorities possess substantial discretion to impose rules of order and pedagogical restrictions on student activities, [13] but they may not structure or administer such rules to discriminate against student prayer or religious speech. For instance, where schools permit student expression on the basis of genuinely neutral criteria and students retain primary control over the content of their expression, the speech of students who choose to express themselves through religious means such as prayer is not attributable to the state and therefore may not be restricted because of its religious content. [14] Student remarks are not attributable to the state simply because they are delivered in a public setting or to a public audience. [15] As the Supreme Court has explained: "The proposition that schools do not endorse everything they fail to censor is not compli-cated," [16] and the Constitution mandates neutrality rather than hostility toward privately initiated religious expression. [17]

APPLYING THE GOVERNING PRINCIPLES IN PARTICULAR CONTEXTS

Prayer During Noninstructional Time

Students may pray when not engaged in school activities or instruction, subject to the same rules designed to prevent material disruption of the educational program that are applied to other privately initiated expressive activities. Among other things, students may read their Bibles or other scriptures, say grace before meals, and pray or study religious materials with fellow students during recess, the lunch hour, or other noninstructional time to the same extent that they may engage in nonreligious activities. While school authorities may impose rules of order and pedagogical restrictions on student activities, they may not discriminate against student prayer or religious speech in applying such rules and restrictions.

Organized Prayer Groups and Activities

Students may organize prayer groups, religious clubs, and "see you at the pole" gatherings before school to the same extent that students are permitted to organize other non-curricular student activities groups. Such groups must be given the same access to school facilities for assembling as is given to other non-curricular groups, without discrimination because of the religious content of their expression. School authorities possess substantial discretion concerning whether to permit the use of school media for student advertising or announcements regarding non-curricular activities. However, where student groups that meet for nonreligious activities are permitted to advertise or announce

97

their meetings—for example, by advertising in a student newspaper, making announcements on a student activities bulletin board or public address system, or handing out leaflets—school authorities may not discriminate against groups who meet to pray. School authorities may disclaim sponsorship of non-curricular groups and events, provided they administer such disclaimers in a manner that neither favors nor disfavors groups that meet to engage in prayer or religious speech.

Teachers, Administrators and other School Employees

When acting in their official capacities as representatives of the state, teachers, school administrators and other school employees are prohibited by the Establishment Clause from encouraging or discouraging prayer, and from actively participating in such activity with students. Teachers may, however, take part in religious activities where the overall context makes clear that they are not participating in their official capacities. Before school or during lunch, for example, teachers may meet with other teachers for prayer or Bible study to the same extent that they may engage in other conversation or nonreligious activities. Similarly, teachers may participate in their personal capacities in privately sponsored baccalaureate ceremonies.

Moments of Silence

If a school has a "minute of silence" or other quiet periods during the school day, students are free to pray silently, or not to pray, during these periods of time. Teachers and other school employees may neither encourage nor discourage students from praying during such time periods.

Accommodation of Prayer During Instructional Time

It has long been established that schools have the discretion to dismiss students to off-premises religious instruction, provided that schools do not encourage or discourage participation in such instruction or penalize students for attending or not attending. Similarly, schools may excuse students from class to remove a significant burden on their religious exercise, where doing so would not impose material burdens on other students. For example, it would be lawful for schools to excuse Muslim students briefly from class to enable them to fulfill their religious obligations to pray during Ramadan.

Where school officials have a practice of excusing students from class on the basis of parents' requests for accommodation of nonreligious needs, religiously motivated requests for excusal may not be accorded less favorable treatment. In addition, in some circumstances, based on federal or state constitutional law or pursuant to state statutes, schools may be required to make accommodations that relieve substantial burdens on students' religious exercise. Schools officials are therefore encouraged to consult with their attorneys regarding such obligations.

Religious Expression and Prayer in Class Assignments

Students may express their beliefs about religion in homework, artwork and other written and oral assignments free from discrimination based on the religious content of their submissions. Such home and classroom work should be judged by ordinary academic standards of substance and relevance and against other legitimate pedagogical concerns identified by the school. Thus, if a teacher's assignment involves writing a poem, the work of a student who submits a poem in the form of a prayer (for example, a psalm) should be judged on the basis of academic standards (such as literary quality) and neither penalized nor rewarded on account of its religious content.

Student Assemblies and Extracurricular Events

Student speakers at student assemblies and extracurricular activities such as sporting events may not be selected on a basis that either favors or disfavors religious speech. Where student speakers are selected on the basis of genuinely neutral, evenhanded criteria and retain primary control over the content of their expression, that expression is not attributable to the school and therefore may not be restricted because of its religious (or anti-religious) content. By contrast, where school officials determine or substantially control the content of what is expressed, such speech is attributable to the school and may not include prayer or other specifically religious (or anti-religious) content. To avoid any mistaken perception that a school endorses student speech that is not in fact attributable to the school, school officials may make appropriate, neutral disclaimers to clarify that such speech (whether religious or nonreligious) is the speaker's and not the school's.

Prayer at Graduation

School officials may not mandate or organize prayer at graduation or select speakers for such events in a manner that favors religious speech such as prayer. Where students or other private graduation speakers are selected on the basis of genuinely neutral, evenhanded criteria and retain primary control over the content of their expression, however, that expression is not attributable to the school and therefore may not be restricted because of its religious (or anti-religious) content. To avoid any mistaken perception that a school endorses student or other private speech that is not in fact attributable to the school, school officials may make appropriate, neutral disclaimers to clarify that such speech (whether religious or nonreligious) is the speaker's and not the school's.

Baccalaureate Ceremonies

School officials may not mandate or organize religious ceremonies. However, if a school makes its facilities and related services available to other private groups, it must make its facilities and services available on the same terms to organizers of privately sponsored religious baccalaureate ceremonies. In addition, a school may disclaim official endorsement of events sponsored by private groups, provided it does so in a manner that neither favors nor disfavors groups that meet to engage in prayer or religious speech.

NOTES:

[1] The relevant portions of the First Amendment provide: "Congress shall make no law respecting an establishment of religion, or prohibiting the free exercise thereof; or abridging the freedom of speech . . . ." U.S. Const. amend. I. The Supreme Court has held that the Fourteenth Amendment makes these provisions applicable to all levels of government—federal, state and local—and to all types of governmental policies and activities. *See Everson v. Board of Educ.*,

330 U.S. 1 (1947); *Cantwell v. Connecticut*, 310 U.S. 296 (1940). [Return to text]

[2] *See, e.g., Everson*, 330 U.S. at 18 (the First Amendment "requires the state to be a neutral in its relations with groups of religious believers and non-believers; it does not require the state to be their adversary. State power is no more to be used so as to handicap religions than it is to favor them"); *Good News Club v. Milford Cent. Sch.*, 533 U.S. 98 (2001). [Return to text]

[3] *Santa Fe Indep. Sch. Dist. v. Doe*, 530 U.S. 290, 302 (2000) (quoting *Board of Educ. v. Mergens*, 496 U.S. 226, 250 (1990) (plurality opinion)); *accord Rosenberger v. Rector of Univ. of Virginia*, 515 U.S. 819, 841 (1995). [Return to text]

[4] *Engel v. Vitale*, 370 U.S. 421 (1962) (invalidating state laws directing the use of prayer in public schools); *School Dist. of Abington Twp. v. Schempp*, 374 U.S. 203 (1963) (invalidating state laws and policies requiring public schools to begin the school day with Bible readings and prayer); *Mergens*, 496 U.S. at 252 (plurality opinion) (explaining that "a school may not itself lead or direct a religious club"). The Supreme Court has also held, however, that the study of the Bible or of religion, when presented objectively as part of a secular program of education (e.g., in history or literature classes), is consistent with the First Amendment. *See Schempp*, 374 U.S. at 225. [Return to text]

[5] *See Lee v. Weisman*, 505 U.S. 577, 599 (1992); *see also Wallace v. Jaffree*, 472 U.S. 38 (1985). [Return to text]

[6] *See Weisman*, 505 U.S. at 587. [Return to text]

[7] 505 U.S. 577 (1992). [Return to text]

[8] 530 U.S. 290 (2000). [Return to text]

[9] *Tinker v. Des Moines Indep. Community Sch. Dist.*, 393 U.S. 503, 506 (1969). [Return to text]

[10] *Capitol Square Review & Advisory Bd. v. Pinette*, 515 U.S. 753, 760 (1995). [Return to text]

[11] *Santa Fe*, 530 U.S. at 302 (explaining that "not every message" that is "authorized by a government policy and take[s] place on government property at government-sponsored school-related events" is "the government's own"). [Return to text]

[12] *Santa Fe*, 530 U.S. at 313. [Return to text]

[13] For example, the First Amendment permits public school officials to review student speeches for vulgarity, lewdness, or sexually explicit language. *Bethel Sch. Dist. v. Fraser*, 478 U.S. 675, 683-86 (1986). Without more, however, such review does not make student speech attributable to the state. [Return to text]

[14] *Rosenberger v. Rector of Univ. of Virginia*, 515 U.S. 819 (1995); *Board of Educ. v. Mergens*, 496 U.S. 226 (1990); *Good News Club v. Milford Cent. Sch.*, 533 U.S. 98 (2001); *Lamb's Chapel v. Center Moriches Union Free Sch. Dist.*, 508 U.S. 384 (1993); *Widmar v. Vincent*, 454 U.S. 263 (1981); *Santa Fe*, 530 U.S. at 304 n.15. In addition, in circumstances where students are entitled to pray, public schools may not restrict or censor their prayers on the ground that they might be deemed "too religious" to others. The Establishment Clause prohibits state officials from making judgments about what constitutes an appropriate prayer, and from favoring or disfavoring certain types of prayers—be they "nonsectarian" and "nonproselytizing" or the opposite—over others. *See Engel v. Vitale*, 370 U.S. 421, 429-30 (1962) (explaining that "one of the greatest dangers to the freedom of the individual to worship in his own way lay in the Government's placing its official stamp of approval upon one particular kind of prayer or one particular form of religious services," that "neither the power nor the prestige" of state officials may "be used to control, support or influence the kinds of prayer the American people can say," and that the state is "without power to prescribe by law any

particular form of prayer"); *Weisman*, 505 U.S. at 594. [Return to text]

[15] *Santa Fe*, 530 U.S. at 302; *Mergens*, 496 U.S. at 248-50. [Return to text]

[16] *Mergens*, 496 U.S. at 250 (plurality opinion); *id.* at 260-61 (Kennedy, J., concurring in part and in judgment). [Return to text

[17] *Rosenberger*, 515 U.S. at 845-46; *Mergens*, 496 U.S. at 248 (plurality opinion); *id.* at 260-61 (Kennedy, J., concurring in part and in judgment). [Return to text]

www.ed.gov/policy/gen/guid/religionandschools/prayer_guidance.html.

RESOURCES

Resources mentioned in this book plus others

"Armadillo Jim" - www.ArmadilloJim.com or
   www.PutOnYourArmor.org

"Armor Crusade" and school outreach
   www.PutOnYourArmor.org or www.ArmadilloJim.com

A Weekend to Remember for couples / Family Life / Dennis and
   Barbara Rainey /- www.familylife.com

AAPHERD programs / award ceremonies / Hoops for the
   Heart™ and Jump Rope for the Heart™ - www.aahperd.org

America's God and Country by Bill Federer -
   www.amerisearch.net - www.americanminute.com

American Alliance for Health, Physical Education, Recreation and
   Dance - www.aahperd.org

American Association of Christian Counselors - www.aacc.net

American Cancer Society annual Relay for Life - www.cancer.org

American Center for Law and Justice - Jay Sekulow -
   www.aclj.org

American Heart Association - www.americanheart.org

American Minute by Bill Federer - www.amerisearch.net

American Petroleum Institute - www.api.org

Armadillo Derby™ - www.PutOnYourArmor.org or
   www.ArmadilloJim.com

AYUSA Global Youth Exchange - www.ayusa.org

Bible Literacy Project - www.bibleliteracy.org

Big Brother or Big Sister - www.bbbs.org

Bill Federer - www.amerisearch.net - www.americanminute.com

Bob Harrison / Known worldwide as Dr. Increase - www.increase.org

Bound 4 Life - http://bound4life.com

Box tops for Education - www.boxtops4education.com

Boy Scouts of America - www.scouting.org

.
Brad and Susanne Ducas- Reclaiming Your School book- Pacific Center for Justice www.pacificjustice.org/resources/bookbroch/

Bridging the Gap - www.crossingsokc.org

Campus Crusade for Christ - www.campuscrusade.com

Center for Law and Religious Freedom of the Christian Legal Society - www.clsnet.org

Champions for Christ - www.championsfc.com

Champions for Christ - www.championsfc.com

ChiAlpha Ministries - www.chialpha.com

Chic-Fil-A® - www.chick-fil-a.com

Child Evangelism Fellowship - www.cefonline.com

Child Evangelism Fellowship - after school Bible Clubs called the Good News Club - www.cefonline.com

Children's Ministry - www.childrensministry.com

Christian Business Leaders / Dr. Increase / Bob Harrison - www.increase.org

Christian Educators Association International - both public and private school teachers - www.ceai.org

Christian Educators Association International - www.raiseyourhand.us

Coca-cola / maker of Dasani - www.cokecce.com

Communities in School - www.cisnet.org

Concert and speakers / public school - www.gospelartists.com

Constitutionally Protected Prayer in Public Elementary and Secondary Schools
www.ed.gov/policy/gen/guid/religionandschools/prayer_guidance.html

Cooks in Schools - www.cooksinschools.org

Counselors to America's Small Business - www.score.org

Creation Evidence Exhibit / Dr. Karl Baugh - www.creationevidence.org

Critical Incident Stress Management - website is www.icisf.org or Melissa Slagle at Livingsolutions@sbcglobal.net

Critical Incident Stress Management trainer / Melissa Slagle / Living Solutions - Livingsolutions@sbcglobal.net

Crossings Community Church - www.crossingsokc.org

Daughters of Heaven purity conference / Suzanne Rentz - www.daughtersofheaven.org

David Barton - www.wallbuilders.com

Dennis and Barbara Rainey / Family Life / A Weekend to Remember for couples - www.familylife.com

Helping Public Schools

Department of Education - www.ed.gov

Department of Education Guidelines -
www.ed.gov/policy/gen/guid/religionandschools/prayer_guidance.html

Diabetes community programs -
www.diabetes.org/support-the-cause/community-campaign.jsp

Diabetes Foundation's School walk -
http://schoolwalk.diabetes.org or www.diabetes.org

Dr. Gary Smalley / Marriage resources -
www.dnaofrelationships.com

Dr. D. James Kennedy - www.reclaimamerica.org

Dr. Increase / Bob Harrison - www.increase.org

Dr. Nasir Siddiki – Wisdom Ministries -
www.wisdom-ministries.com

Exchange student programs - www.ayusa.org

Family Life / Dennis and Barbara Rainey / A Weekend to
Remember for couples - www.familylife.com

Family Life Today - www.familylife.com

Fellowship of Christian Athletes - www.FCA.org

Fellowship of Christian Athletes - www.fca.org

Flags - www.flags.com

Focus on the Family - www.family.org

Gary Smalley / Marriage resources -
www.dnaofrelationships.com

Geology Society - www.geosociety.org

George Lucas Foundation - Edutopia www.edutopia.org

Gideon's - www.gideons.org

Girl Scouts of America - www.girlscouts.org

Gospel Music Association - www.gmamusicawards.com

Graduation - www.projectgraduation.org

Grammy® Foundation and the Dove Awards® programs / scholarships and partnership - www.grammy.com

Grief Recovery Institute - www.grief-recovery.com

Grief recovery project / assembly - www.icriedtoo.org

Guidance on Constitutionally Protected Prayer in Public Elementary and Secondary Schools
www.ed.gov/policy/gen/guid/religionandschools/prayer_guidance.html

Harrison House Publishing - www.harrisonhouse.com

Harry and Cheryl Salem - Mourning to Morning book - www.salemfamilyministries.org

Helping Public Schools - www.helpingpublicschools.com

Homeland Security - www.dhs.gov

I Believe® campaign - www.ibelievethemovement.com

I Cried Too book, CD and plush bunny - www.icriedtoo.org

I Cried Too grief recovery project/assembly - www.icriedtoo.org

In His Grip golf tournament - www.inhisgripgolf.com

International Association of Fairs and Expositions - www.fairsandexpos.com

John Mason's - An Enemy Called Average book - www.freshword.com

Josh McDowell - www.josh.org

Juvenile Diabetes Research Foundation - www.jdrf.org

Kids All American Fishing - www.kids-fishing.com

Kids for Christ Bible Club - www.kfcusa.org

Laugh Your Way to a Happy Marriage / weekend encounter - www.laughyourway.com

Life After Death book by Rev. Tony Cooke - www.tonycooke.org

Lions Club - www.lionsclubs.org

Living Solutions / Melissa Slagle / CISM trainer - Livingsolutions@sbcglobal.net

Madalyn Murray O'Hair's son - William J. Murray,- Religious Freedom Coalition - www.rfcnet.org

Make A Difference Day - www.makeadifferenceday.com

March of Dimes - www.marchofdimes.com

Marriage enrichment / Laugh Your Way to a Happy Marriage - www.laughyourway.com

Marriage resources / Dr. Gary Smalley - www.dnaofrelationships.com

Melissa Slagle / CISM trainer / Living Solutions - Livingsolutions@sbcglobal.net

Mothers Against Drunk Drivers - www.madd.org

Mourning to Morning book - by Rev. Harry and Cheryl Salem - www.salemfamilyministries.org

Nasir Siddiki – Wisdom Ministries - www.wisdom-ministries.com

National Association of Restaurant Owners -
www.restaurant.org

National Association of Student Councils - www.nasc.us

National Center for Education Statistics - www.nces.ed.gov

National Christian Counselors Association - www.ncca.org

National Church Adopt-A-School Initiative, or NCAASI strategy
Project Turn•Around Implementation Toolkit* -
www.TonyEvans.org

National Council on Bible Curriculum in Public Schools
(NCBCPS) President and Founder, Elizabeth Ridenour and
endorsed by Mr. and Mrs. Chuck Norris -
www.bibleinschools.net

National Day of Prayer - www.ndptf.org

National Education Association - www.nea.org/teacherday

National Honor Society - www.nhs.us

National Principal of the Year - www.principals.org

National Right to Life - www.nrlc.org

National School Lunch Week / National School Nutrition Association - www.schoolnutrition.org

National School Nutrition Association -
www.schoolnutrition.org

National School Safety Center - www.schoolsafety.us

National Speakers Association - www.nsaspeaker.org

NFL Youth Football programs - www.nflyouthfootball.com

Noah's Ark stage production - www.noahtickets.com

Nutrition - www.schoolnutrition.org

Nutrition Association - www.schoolnutrition.org
    Oilfield Christian Fellowship -
    www.OilfieldChristianFellowship.com

Operation Angle Tree - Prison Fellowship Ministry -
    www.angeltree.org

Peter Enn, poet - www.agoodword.net/america2.htm

Peter Marshall Ministries - www.petermarshallministries.com

Points of Light Foundation - www.pointsoflight.org

President's Council on Physical Fitness - www.fitness.gov

Principal of the Year - www.principals.org

Prison Fellowship Ministry - Operation Angle Tree -
    www.pfm.org

Project Graduation party - www.projectgraduation.org

Protected Prayer in Public Elementary and Secondary Schools -
    www.ed.gov/policy/gen/guid/religionandschools/prayer_guidance.html

Prudential Spirit of Community Awards - www.principals.org

Punt, Pass & Kick® competition - www.nflyouthfootball.com

Purity conference for young ladies / Suzanne Rentz -
    www.daughtersofheaven.org

Put On Your Armor - "Armadillo Jim" -
    www.PutOnYourArmor.org or www.ArmadilloJim.com

Reclaim America - www.reclaimamerica.org

Reclaim Your School - book -
    http://www.pacificjustice.org/resources/bookbroch/

Recycling associations - www.nrc-recycle.org

Religious Freedom Coalition - William J. Murray, (son of
    Madalyn Murray O'Hair) www.rfcnet.org

Religious Freedom Day - www.religiousfreedomday.com

Rotary International - www.rotary.org

Rule books with your insignia on the cover -
    www.everyrule.com/sports_az_list.html

School assemblies - www.schoolshows.com

School Bus Fleet - www.schoolbusfleet.com

School Nutrition Association / National School Lunch Week -
    www.schoolnutrition.org

Schoolife - www.schoolife.org

See You At the Pole - www.syatp.com

Society of Petroleum Engineers - www.spe.org

Speakers / public school - www.armadillojim.com and
    www.gospelartists.com

Standard and Poor's / research information about public schools
    - www.schoolmatters.com

Teacher of the Year -
    www.ccsso.org/projects/national_teacher_of_the_year
    (spaces have underscore)

Teachers Religion in Public Schools- www.clsnet.org

Teen Mania - www.teenmania.com

The American Legion - www.legion.org

The Church's Response Following A Disaster / Melissa Slagle -
Livingsolutions@sbcglobal.net
Toastmasters International - www.toastmasters.org

Tony Cooke - Life After Death book - www.tonycooke.org

Tour de Cure bike ride - Visit: www.tour.diabetes.org

USDA Animal Welfare / licensed agents, animal handlers,
animal edutainment or exhibitors -
www.aphis.usda.gov/ac/publications.html

Edutopia -learning opportunities: http://www.edutopia.org

Wall Builders - America's forgotten history and heroes -
David Barton - www.wallbuilders.com

When Children Grieve book - www.grief-recovery.com

William J. Murray, (son of Madalyn Murray O'Hair) - Religious
Freedom Coalition www.rfcnet.org

Wisdom Ministries / Dr. Nasir Siddiki -
www.wisdom-ministries.com

World Harvest Resources - www.harvestresources.com

YoungLife - www.younglife.org

Youth for Christ - www.yfc.org

Author Contact Information

Web Sites

www.HelpingPublicSchools.com
www.PutOnYourArmor.org
www.ArmadilloJim.com
www.ICriedToo.org

E-mail your success stories and your
innovative ideas in helping
public schools to:

jim@armadillojim.com

NOTES

NOTES

NOTES

NOTES